Re-examining
THE ART OF SALES

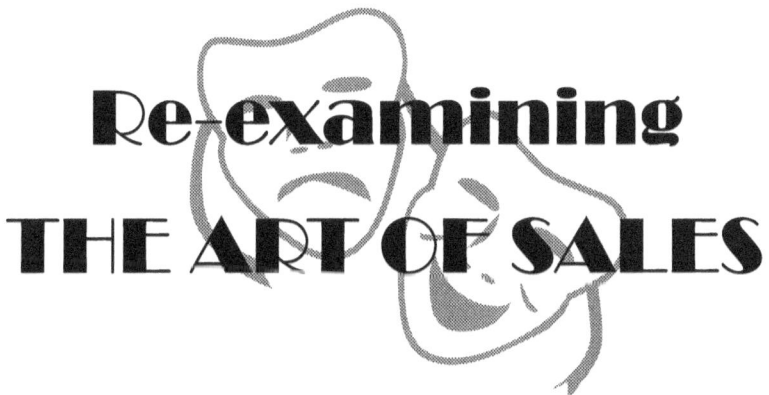

Broadway Style

by

Nilton De Macedo, M.Ed.

Bloomington, IN   authorHOUSE™   Milton Keynes, UK

AuthorHouse™
1663 Liberty Drive, Suite 200
Bloomington, IN 47403
www.authorhouse.com
Phone: 1-800-839-8640

AuthorHouse™ UK Ltd.
500 Avebury Boulevard
Central Milton Keynes, MK9 2BE
www.authorhouse.co.uk
Phone: 08001974150

This book is a work of non-fiction. Unless otherwise noted, the author and the publisher make no explicit guarantees as to the accuracy of the information contained in this book and in some cases, names of people and places have been altered to protect their privacy.

First published by AuthorHouse 6/7/2006

ISBN: 1-4259-3807-8 (e)
ISBN: 1-4259-3809-4 (sc)

Library of Congress Control Number: 2006904433

Printed in the United States of America
Bloomington, Indiana

This book is printed on acid-free paper.

A tremendous amount of preparatory work and continuous training is necessary to turn your vague wish into a professional excellence, so that in the end you are not a wunderkind [genius], or a talent dilettante [amateur], but a master of your craft.

ALEXANDER Y. TAIROV (1885-1950)
Notes of a Director - 1921

Contents

Acknowledgements

Although my name is the only one on the cover of this book, I couldn't take full credit for all the information within. It's easy to notice that my ideas are a mosaic of opinions from different sources, including influence from co-workers with different backgrounds, as well as mentors who decided to help me succeed despite my shortcomings, my fears, and my inexperience.

My wife and children have always played a big role in my life. They have always considered me a success, and offered full support even when I was struggling with life-changing decisions. Our son, Moroni, volunteered to proof the originals and has offered many constructive suggestions to improve text flow and clarity.

On the professional side, I could not forget my first boss in the U.S., Stuart Wheelwright, or his late wife, Kim, as well as Will Thompson, a great co-worker, among many others. They were fundamental in helping my family and I assimilate the American culture, and made us feel at home in our adopted country. They are eternal members in my personal Hall of Fame.

Within the real estate scene, everything started with my first broker, Greg Masters, who taught me the need for self-discipline in the road to success. On the same level I'm appreciative of Doug Yeaman, whom I quote in this book (without his permission!). He taught me some of the sales techniques that I now accept as essential to success. I've tried hard to incorporate most of them in my day-to-day work since our first encounter, about ten years ago.

Last, but not least, I'll be forever thankful to my company's top management, John Brown, Shawn Janke and Max Thompson, who have descended the corporate ladder to my level and taken the time to motivate me financially and emotionally to make this book jump from dream to reality.

Foreword

I had the chance to examine the original notes that were the basis for this book, and I liked what I read.

"RE-EXAMINING THE ART OF SALES" is a must read book for Realtors® at all levels of experience. In fact it's a handbook that every sales professional should keep at his or her fingertips.

As a Real Estate Broker myself, I have to deal with training of new and seasoned agents on a daily basis. The trick is to simplify the training and present it in an easy to understand format. This book does exactly that.

Nilton has captured an understandable way of relating sales training in this unique "Broadway" format. Of equal importance is the fact that this book sticks to the basics and not only covers sales techniques but also the emotions involved. Conceived out of necessity to motivate sales agents in his native homeland, the principles and techniques raised the bar on professionalism and ethics in Brazil and will do the same for anyone that reads it.

Congratulations, Nilton. I wish you the best success.

John Brown
- *Branch Manager - Coldwell Banker Residential Brokerage (North Davis, Utah office)*
- *2005 President of the Weber-North Davis Association of Realtors®.*

Preface

Since I was a little boy, I had a dream of being an actor. I loved watching TV or going to the movies and putting myself in the actor's position. In my mind, I could easily act just like them. In my childish way, I thought it didn't take much to be a good actor. All they were doing was "making believe" and – as most children – I was an expert at that! Little did I know that acting is more than pretending! It's really getting inside a character, thinking like it, behaving like it… living their lives!

At age 5 I got second place modeling a Mardi Gras costume during "Carnival" in Rio de Janeiro. The cash prize was good enough to help my parents clear a few minor debts. At 7, I performed at the County Fair and presented a 15-minute long monologue. I showed up dressed as an old man who talked about the "good, old days" and how he missed them. When, with 8 years of age, I wrote and directed a couple of short 15 minutes plays (having the neighbors' children as actors who performed them a few times to an audience of 20 to 25 grown-ups at a time). Everybody had thought that playwriting, directing or acting was my certain future.

Of course, I didn't grow to be an actor. Instead of taking acting classes, I majored in Mass Communications, and minored in Marketing, Publicity and Public Relations. In Brazil, where I was born, I went on to become involved in real estate still in my college years. When I moved to the United States, in 1986, I decided to continue to work as a sales specialist.

Did I give up my future as an actor? In some sense, I did, but in a broader sense, I didn't. Sales and acting are intertwined. We "incorporate" a character when we sell, and it is that same character (not ourselves) that actually interacts with our clients. If we really think about it, "selling is acting". A good salesman does nothing else than sell his ability to represent a personage and convince the audience.

The world itself is a stage and all of us are actors here. We are associated with acting – consciously or sub-consciously. We perform several roles at home, school, the work place, and in social functions… We try to act our best with our friends, spouses, bosses, subordinates, etc.

Usually, in these situations, we are performing naturally, but when it comes to perform on stage, TV, or films, it takes lots of energy, concentration, presence of mind, and skill. However, in no other profession we depend on a good performance to earn our daily bread as we do in sales.

To those who don't believe they have a character that they play when talking to clients, think again! What kind of person is always up beat, happy, enthusiastic, and committed? Sorry to disappoint you but it's the character you chose to represent – not necessarily you! – that has that almost perfect personality.

A salesman who is in financial trouble in his personal life or struggling with marital problems will never convey these situations to a client, while "in character". His character will always be in control, excited about what he has to offer, and ready to empathize with clients in the same predicament, without releasing personal information that can destroy or negatively affect the vision the client has of the professional. His character is successful despite his real financial situation; always emotionally upbeat, and indifferent to the salesman inner feelings. Cold as it may seem, it is the way to success and top production.

Are there many similarities between selling and acting? I surely believe so! This book's intent is to compare the two careers and establish important points that anybody involved with sales may learn from actors and actresses.

Consider our clients as the audience. Start viewing salespeople as the actors and actresses themselves. Compare the sales managers with the director and the company owner (or stock holders) as the producer.

Can you see the similarities?

NOTE: *To keep with the "show biz" theme throughout this book some words may have been used to replace common terms, such as:*

> AUDIENCE *has sometimes been used instead of* CLIENTS,
> ACTOR *and/or* CHARACTER *instead of* SALESMAN,
> PLAY *instead of* SALES PRESENTATION,
> DIRECTOR *instead of* SALES MANAGER.

At the same time, In order to avoid going over the top with "political correctness" I decided not to include gender variations, therefore, some words like salesman, he, him, and his also mean saleswoman, she, her and hers, respectively.

Comparison Charts

–Actors vs. Salespeople

IN SHOW BUSINESS	IN THE SALES ARENA
ACTORS are expected to entertain and communicate with people through their performing of dramatic roles. Only a few actors achieve recognition as stars on the stage, in motion pictures, or on television. A somewhat larger number are well known, experienced performers, who frequently are cast in supporting roles. Most actors struggle for a toehold in the profession and pick up parts wherever they can. Many successful actors continue to accept small roles, including commercials and product endorsements. Some actors employed by theater companies teach acting courses to the public in general.	SALESPEOPLE present a product, service or idea, through an emotional sales presentation carefully defined. Only a few salespeople achieve recognition as top producers. A somewhat large number are well known, experienced sales people, with average sales figures, who somehow never step up to be a top producer. Most salespeople struggle for a satisfying job, and may accept any positions available in the market. Many successful salespeople continue to combine different part-time jobs and, in some cases, extremely conflicting projects. If employed full time, they also manage to conduct seminars, training classes, etc.

–Directors vs. Sales Managers

IN SHOW BUSINESS	IN THE SALES ARENA
DIRECTORS interpret plays or scripts. In addition, they audition and select cast members, conduct rehearsals, and direct the work of the cast and crew. Directors use their know-how in acting, voice, and movement to reach the best possible performance and usually approve the scenery, costumes, music, and choreography.	SALES MANAGERS oversee the sales force. In addition, they recruit new salespeople, conduct consistent training, and direct the work of the sales crew. Sales Managers use their knowledge of sales, proven techniques and motivation to promote the best possible performance. They usually also stress the need for grooming, practice, and skills.

–Producers vs. Company Owners

IN SHOW BUSINESS	IN THE SALES ARENA
PRODUCERS should be seen, in reality, as entrepreneurs. They select plays or scripts, arrange financing, and decide on the size and content of the production and its budget. They hire directors, principal members of the cast, key production staff members, and they negotiate contracts with artistic personnel, often in accordance with collective bargaining agreements. Producers also coordinate the activities of writers, directors, managers, and other personnel.	COMPANY OWNERS are basically entrepreneurs. They select the methods and the guidelines, oversee the finances, and decide the size on contents of the production (product line) and its budget. They hire Sales Managers, the principal members of the company, key production staff members, and negotiate contracts with other employees, often in accordance with employment laws. They also coordinate the jobs of most marketing personnel, managers, etc.

Two points of view

1) Qualification, Presentation and Negotiation:

I like to break up the sales process into three major groups:

Qualification,

Presentation, and

Negotiation.

Each of them can encompass sub-groups, but to me, they all end up in one of these three major categories.

Qualification is twofold:

- Qualification of the client, including the initial analysis of each prospect, the first contact – in person or by phone – the ice-breaking, and other initial stages; and
- Qualification of the salesman, including his personal training, personal preparation, and self-conditioning.

Presentation encompasses the main phase of the sales process, when (face-to-face with the client) we demonstrate our product, service, or idea and our interest in servicing them from that point on.

Negotiation covers the meeting of the minds, the confrontation between the client's expectations, and our ability to fulfill them. Its climax is the closing, which has been defined as the main objective in the sales process.

2) Rehearsal, Performance, and Critique:

Comparing with the theatrical world, the sales process would more or less fit into the three phases of performance:

- Rehearsal,
- Performance, and
- Critic's Review.

Rehearsal takes in consideration the preparation the salesman goes through in order to maximize his effectiveness. It represents the off-scene activity; the efforts that are not seen by the client, but that will benefit him afterwards.

Performance is the sales presentation itself, the moment of personal interaction and relationship. It is certainly the longest and the most climactic of all three.

Critique (review) takes in consideration the post-performance activities, in which the client will measure the delivery against the promises. It will ultimately define the successfulness of the sale, and it becomes the base for adjustments in future presentations. In sales it can be brought up by self-analysis, review (sales reports) or comments – positive or not – from the clients.

The following common points comparing acting and selling will be classified according to these two major groups. It's my understanding that this logical arrangement will help us visualize their importance and their position in the big picture.

It all comes down to **Preparation** (Qualification or Rehearsal), **Demonstration** (Performance or Presentation of our product or services), and **Conciliation** (Negotiation or Critique). This is the sales cycle that goes on and on and on…

	Qualification	Presentation	Negotiation
Rehearsal	**QR**	**PR**	**NR**
Performance	**QP**	**PP**	**NP**
Critique	**QC**	**PC**	**NC**

⬇	⬇	⬇
Preparation	*Demonstration*	*Conciliation*

Acting and Selling – the common points

1) Preparation

	Qualification	Presentation	Negotiation
Rehearsal	**QR**	PR	NR
Performance	**QP**	PP	NP
Critique	**QC**	PC	NC

The traditional greek masks show the duality of the theater (sales); comedy and drama (buying and selling)

There are two main divisions in the sales process, which are actually parts of the same process. In order to be most effective the salesman should handle them differently. They are:

- Buying
- Selling

Learning to recognize the difference becomes fundamental in a salesman's life, if he is interested in living a successful career.

Experiment asking a salesman to explain the difference. Listen carefully! Most won't know the difference, which may explain why salesmen talk too much. Wouldn't they be trying to cover up their ignorance in what seems to be a basic question?

Buying and selling are two different sides of the same coin.

Selling takes place when the salesman causes the prospect to become aware of a need or a want discovered by the salesman. Then, after the salesman has persuaded the prospect that his product, idea or service is the one that best fulfill that need or want, the selling process is completed!

Stanford Research Institute (SRI) has found that a person's earnings potential is based 12.5% on knowledge and 87.5% on people skills. Learning how to adapt your unique selling technique to each of your prospect's buying styles can increase your people skills effectiveness by up to 300%.

In many cases, a sales manager could exponentially increase the amount of business by helping their salespeople recognize the need to consistently follow proven sales techniques and use them to motivate their customers to recognize their need for our products, services or ideas.

In the professional selling game the difference between selling and buying must always be recognized. There is absolutely no sense in proceeding with the entire selling process when a person is ready to buy, except to interest the client in buying additional products or services.

When the prospect or customer recognizes his need or want, all the salesman has to do is clearly point out that particular need and want and make sure it what the prospect sees. Next, he is to present his proposition as the best answer, call for the action, and complete the sale. It's EASY TO SAY, but without self-discipline may be DIFFICULT TO DO.

It is imperative for the professional salesman to understand that this process exists and then become skillful and proficient in performing it, constantly refine the process, and improve the results. Very few — very, very few — people in the sales profession understand and master this process. Knowing the process will guide the salesman to discover how to recover when the selling process is breaking down. If the salesman has not studied the process, hasn't become skillful at every aspect of it, and hasn't mastered how to recover from failures, then he will never become the salesman he could be.

Don't ignore the details

Anybody can see the whole picture. In a play we can re-count the story and describe the characters personality, but sometimes we don't remember the character's clothes or how many times the main character left the scene during the whole show.

In sales, we are supposed to pay attention to some critical details because they sometimes hide the clue to which direction we may take our presentation. We should take notice, among other things, of the following:

What part of the presentation creates a sparkle of enthusiasm and acceptance, and emphasize that point.

Specific comments that undercover the client's needs and wants in relation to our product or services.

Shortcomings (like hearing impairment, short attention span, or comprehension); strengths (previous knowledge of our product/ service, or a strong rapport).

General signs of acceptance.

If talking to two or more people, we should notice who is the least interested and involve him. We may do it directly or create a situation where the most interest party does the selling for us.

Much time and effort could be saved if we stay alert to those details. It may sound overwhelming to pay attention to our presentation and at the same time watch for specific signs from our clients. In time, as we master some basic scripts, it becomes natural and actually interesting to play this double role. All we are doing, as we present our message, is "testing the waters" as we go on with the presentation. We may, accordingly, quote past client's feelings and reactions, or change the tone of our voice, our body language, or speech speed.

There is plenty of free information that our clients are going to volunteer if we only pay attention. This information sometimes guarantees a closing, that otherwise could pass unnoticed. If we avoid second-guessing and get the facts, straight from the client, we will be much better off.

The tools of the trade

Selling, like any craft, requires some tools – things we can use to do our job.

When we talk about tools, the first things that come to our minds are electronic gadgets that will help us perform the basic tasks of our job, such as cell phones, faxes, computers, wireless e-mail, GPS, etc. Those are indispensable partners to any successful salesperson. However, the tools we are talking about are internal and co-exist with the professional. These tools are essential in making the salesman guide the audience to accept his point of view, and follow his directions in a meaningful, non-threatening way.

A top-producer professional will guide the audience to closing by means of the same tools commonly used in the show business, such as the voice, appearance and body movement. These are to the salespeople (and the actor) what paint, canvas, and brushes are to the painter. Anyone can go out and buy the basic tools of painting. Not everybody can paint! Everyone has a voice. Not everyone can impress the client to make a decision.

Other internal tools are also important, such as imagination, sensitivity, intelligence, self-control, empathy, and patience. Every good salesman relies on these internal tools as much as the external tools. The better the actor, the more he makes use of all his tools, internal and external.

A common misconception is that regional, foreign accents, or small speech impairment(s) may stop short a sales career. I use my foreign accent as a good icebreaker. Most clients are dying to know where I'm from, how I moved to the U.S., and what do I think of my adopted country. I go with the flow and answer all the questions honest and directly. This open conversation usually becomes the foundation of a great business relationship.

For better results, salespeople (and actors) must love themselves (I'm great! I'm amazing!). This behavior may be criticized in Hollywood, where egotistic actors think they are only two or three steps below godliness, but this same behavior – with the right dosage of self-control, of course – will set the base for a successful career in sales.

Similarly, nobody will ever achieve real success unless they like what they're doing. What you do is more important than how much you make. How you feel about what you do is more important than what you do. The more you love what you're doing, the more successful it will be for you. Never set compensation as your goal. Find work you like, and the compensation will follow. You don't pay the price of success. You enjoy the profits for success. As the actor's objective is to serve the author's intention, the salesman's objective should be to represent the product's value, and the company's master plan. By using the tools of his trade he can do so.

Developing a routine that involves relaxing and working

It's obvious to anybody how stressful is an actors life. Maybe that's why "they get the big bucks". Also, that would explain the many cases of alcohol and drug abuse, divorce, depression, and suicide, among other terrible consequences of not dealing with stress satisfactorily.

Some of us generally tend to consider relaxation to be a waste of precious time. We simply do not put high value on relaxation. We evaluate ourselves more on measurable things such as personal achievements and financial worth – not emotional wellness. We often tend to feel guilty if we aren't constantly being productive.

This sense of guilt usually arises from our parents' pre-adolescence brainwashing. They taught us to achieve and perform... to continuously strive to become Superman. I know what you're thinking, "Yeah, well, I do sometimes have problems unwinding, but it's not going to kill me." Think again, because it actually could.

According to medical experts, stress has become a major health problem. It has been linked to heart disease, high blood pressure, stroke, cancer, and other serious illnesses. The solution is to learn *how* to unwind. This learning process, however, is not easy – especially if you're the stern, workaholic, and achievement-oriented type.

There are a number of basic rules to help you add balance to your life. Begin by seeking out leisurely activities that are separate from work. If you're the "analytical" type (such a lawyer, scientist, accountant, etc...) then pursue relaxation through physically involving activities such as gardening, building a deck or cooking.

Make sure you work up a sweat once in a while. Thirty minutes of intense cardiovascular exercise immediately reduces body tension. Studies have also found that weightlifting counters anxiety, depression, and boosts self-esteem. This can be also achieved with aerobics as well.

Also, choose a relaxing activity that *you* consider relaxing. If a friend wants to go fishing and you know you'll get bored quickly, then don't go. Boredom often adds to stress levels as opposed to diminishing them.

Obviously, above it all, you must assign little breaks in your busy schedule.

Using other people's money, ideas, and efforts

If we could ask the most successful people, "What's your secret?" They would certainly acknowledge, "There is a secret, and it is called OPM – other people's money."

Most top achievers invested their energies in taking great ideas (in some cases someone else's ideas) and conceptualizing great projects or companies around them. The next step is to go out and get other people to fund those ideas. It is very curious that even after they have plenty of their own funds, they still feel it would be somehow like cheating if they fund things themselves. They need the validation that comes from convincing someone else to put their money into their endeavor.

There is no doubt that OPM has been a major force in business. It shows even more clearly in commissioned sales. In order for a salesperson to accomplish their goals, they take advantage of their company's money and/or ideas (in the form of supplies, utilities, facilities, and promotional ads, products, services, programs, client base, scripts, etc.), offering only their personal efforts and time. The goal of both company and salesperson is to accomplish their common goals. This contribution to the equation, however small, is key to the process. Salespeople can't do it all, but it's obvious that companies would not succeed without their sales force. This creates a symbiotic existence with equal benefits to both parties.

Besides using other people's money and ideas, the ultimate goal of successful people is actually get to the point of having their efforts delegated to others, making their own use of time more productive. They use assistants, computer software, agencies, and so forth, to speed up the results and minimize their efforts. In such a competitive market, where a regular workday seems to be shorter and shorter, this ability to share the burden is the true mark of a winner.

Don't wait for a director (sales manager) to tell you everything

First, he doesn't have the time. Second, their job is not really to baby-sit you for the rest of your life. A great sales manager I worked with insisted that we should make our own decisions whenever he wasn't readily available. His favorite line was "ask for forgiveness, rather than permission". The actor must be courageous to go ahead and make mistakes, always being aware that most of the time the audience won't even notice.

If you find yourself into a treacherous situation, try to get out of it all by yourself. Have in mind that the audience likes when characters overcome difficulties. I wouldn't be surprised if someday we find out that some clients, on purpose, have put us in strange situations in order to judge our ability to deal with disaster.

As dangerous as it looks, however, a salesman that is careful to protect the company's policy will be careful in going out on a limb. While trying to make his point, he will never demonstrate the product in a way that will offend the customer, stain the competitor's image unjustly, or exaggerate to the point of lying. As the actor or actress needs to understand the story and intention of the author, so the salesman is bound to be aware of company goals, policies, and general plans. Getting away from the script is as dangerous as driving without seat belt. Yes, you may never be in an accident, but your chances are now less than ideal if you ever get into one.

No matter how much better than the sales manager we may think we are... chances are we are wrong. Any normal company would never survive too long with a mediocre manager leading the team. If he is in that position and if – hopefully – he has been successful at it, then we better open our eyes and direct our ears to get guidance as we go. I don't know any successful salesman who does not follow the manager's guidelines.

More than the director in a play, Sales Managers can be compared to good coaches. They explain the play, they motivate the players, but then don't touch the ball. It will remain the Sales Associate's goal to follow the guidelines, and use his talent to get to the victory. My favorite analogy – although a little overused – is to imagine that a salesman is someone lost in a forest. The sales manager is the rescue group in a helicopter. From the forest, all we can see are the trees. It becomes hard, if not impossible, to find the way out. The crew in a search and rescue helicopter can see the trails, the natural obstacles. In other words, they can be key to our survival. Sometimes, however, it is up to us to find our way out or perish.

Memorizing scripts – Is it for everybody?

Children, as well as adults, are forced to memorize long scripts in order to be part of a play. If even older actor or actresses can do it, why can't a salesman? I would say that memorizing scripts is sometimes the biggest concern for sales people. They just get overwhelmed with the size of the text and decide not to put the effort. If only there were some helpful tricks... Well, here are some of the ones used in theater that may help us too:

- Read the script over and over and then over again.
- Understand the general idea and form of the presentation before you try memorizing each and every word of the script.
- Use a tape recorder to assist. This system works well if you spend a lot of alone time, like in a car commuting, or between classes. You can also use another person to feed you your cue lines and assist you when you are stuck and can't remember the next lines.
- Try to say your lines in front of a mirror. This way you can practice your expressions as well as your lines.
- Memorize the script in short overlapping pieces. In a long monologue you will likely have lines that are very similar in thought, so the overlapping bits will serve as glue.
- Look for "landmarks" to help you get back on track if you drift off. Landmarks are lines you just can't miss, such as trial closes, questions, strong points and lines that just plain stick out.
- As in theater, keep character. Do not apologize to the client if you forgot the script (they don't know better). Stay cool! Take a calm deep simple breath and then go on.
- Use flash cards. They are portable and don't require batteries.
- Memorize certain movements that may trigger your memory as to what you are to say.

- Look for the objective in each line. Why do I say this? What do I want to accomplish?
- Type or handwrite your script or parts of it and then read it through.
- Read the first sentence aloud from your script. Put down the script and repeat it from short-term memory. Read the second sentence from the script. Repeat it. Repeat the first and second sentences together from memory. Do this until you've memorized a large part, and then repeat it to yourself a number of times.

Another helpful tip is to find out what type of learner you are. When your study for a test, do you recall how the teacher explained it to you? Do you remember certain phrases that you read?

If you are a AUDITORY LEARNER: Record yourself saying the lines and play it back several times a day, while speaking along with the recording as you learn the lines. Also, read the lines out loud whenever you practice them.

VISUAL LEARNER: Read it with a friend (representing your clients). Take note of their expressions when certain lines are said. Visualize where it is in the script as you run lines.

PHYSICAL LEARNER: When you read through your lines, do the gestures as if facing a client.

You may not be just a visual learner or just an auditory learner. Actually, most people are combinations. I suggest that you do all three of these learning techniques.

Despite our efforts, our mind can go blank for no apparent reason (which really happens, even to professionals). If we have the script memorized, it won't take long to get back on track.

Rehearse, do some lab work, practice... but act as if there wasn't any rehearsal

It always bothered me why some salespeople (usually inexperienced rookies) insist on "shooting from the hips". They go to their sales presentation with nothing but "a prayer in their hearts". It also surprises me that they seem to expect some kind of success. Wouldn't it be less stressful and futile to take a few minutes prior to our encounter with a client and mentally review what to say, what to do, check the names, and any other information we may need?

Many years ago I heard of an experiment, which called my attention and gave me a sense of value towards mental practice. Two basketball teams were formed including high school age kids, in preparation for a 3-point competition. One had no training whatsoever prior to the tournament. The other one was trained in a very unconventional way: they practice shooting from the 3-point range, but with no balls. By mimicking the hand movements, they were expected to mentally visualize the shot and act it out as if it was really a real situation. After the competition, the practicing team not only won, but also every player in the group increased their personal scoring averages.

The old musicals with Fred Astaire and company had moments where the stars began to tap dance in such a subtle way that the audience could swear it was just improvised. In order to achieve that "natural" atmosphere, however they would practice over and over until their ankle started hurting, and in some cases, even then the practice would go on.

Nobody discusses the value of stage practice (role playing), but it is not always feasible. Since I heard the experiment I've just mentioned, the idea of mental practice has become one of my goals. Before meeting a client I review the possible objections, the dialogues that may be used, and any comments that may take me by surprise.

This mental rehearsal can be done during a meal, while driving to the appointment, or any other time prior to that encounter. It eases my tension, helps me to focus, and surely diminishes the chances of hearing an objection that I was not prepared for.

Permanently involved in the soldier's discipline

Probably the most difficult thing for a "civilian" (non-salesman) to grasp is the monumental amount of mental and physical work involved. I often meet people who think the hardest thing about selling is the constant traveling. They don't consider the amount of effort that goes in setting up an appointment and the preparation necessary prior to presenting the product.

Just like soldiers, I worked not only under rain, but also under extremely hot temperatures. I remember a few times going for a shower at lunch time, so I didn't look soaked with sweat when it was time to meet my client in the afternoon. Although it shouldn't be the norm, I have visited with some clients while running a small fever or while experiencing earache.

Discipline is to become second nature. We should approach our work as professionally and in as businesslike a manner as a doctor, lawyer or banker. There is no such a thing as a "variable schedule". Obviously we don't do the usual nine-to-five, but we can't afford to re-plan our working hours day by day according to our personal interests.

The best definition of discipline I ever heard is this: doing what is required of you regardless of your problems and fears. With discipline comes courage – courage to extend ourselves, to subdue the voices in our head, which I call our personal demons.

Discipline is courage. No great salesman can overcome the job's pressures without it. The pressures are more than just physical. More than ever the business world is cost and time conscious. Production costs have risen; therefore our productivity must increase exponentially to keep the company healthy. For the salesman, there is little room for deviation.

Whether we feel like facing the clients on a particular day is immaterial. We are expected to show up on time, master our scripts, and be in peak physical shape. Obviously it wouldn't be acceptable to tell a client, "I don't think I feel like seeing you today. Can we do it tomorrow?"

The basic requirements for success are usually strict and unyielding. Regardless of his productivity the salesman is never exempt from the rules for very long. Some people make themselves seem so important that they feel they can't be replaced, even if they don't meet the demands. In reality, salespeople who don't meet the demands ultimately find it difficult to get work.

In order to understand the plot (the sales process as a whole), we may want to work backward

There are a few things we need to do when getting ready to master a product or service presentation. After reading the script three or four times (twice is never enough), pay special attention to the last few pages (the closing). Understand those pages thoroughly. What happens there? What's the subtext? How does each section of the presentation lead to that climactic point? Will each client react differently to the same basic message?

If you get to a point and decide that at that phase of the presentation the client should be sold to your product or service, start checking back in the script for all contributing factors. You will find out a few key points. Go back and look for the breadcrumbs that lead you to where the treasure is.

In order to understand those contributing factors, think of the crucial point of earlier scenes (phases of the presentation). Don't let them pass by unnoticed by the client. Make them savor those points one by one until there is a full comprehension of the message. Observe if the client is digesting the information. Guide them, subliminally, to prepare for the happy ending.

I like to use price conditioning all the way through the presentation to stress the value of a product or service. When a client, early in the presentation, builds an idea of how many benefits your product or service carries with it, as soon as pricing is established, the client won't collapse or act surprised. Considering that price is the most common obstacle to a sale, getting this monster out of the way is a major victory.

Find out in your script a few areas where price conditioning would fit naturally and make each one of those hits in every presentation. As in most of the message, be careful to make those statements matter-of-factly. If you were successful in imposing your expertise in your product or service, your client will take the hint and accept the suggestion as coming from a pro.

The show (sales) must go on

We wrongfully complain that "buyers are liars", but we should also notice that most salespeople are "whiners". We can create the most innovative excuses not to sell. We should understand that it is a major problem… no… it's more like a disease… considering that selling is the main point in our job description.

Besides making excuses, some salespeople (statistically the worst producers) become superstitious beyond measure and critical of the company, the supervisors and other salespeople. Superstition takes the form of "certain days/times/seasons" where business is low, certain client profiles that will not lead to a close, and certain areas that don't yield enough sales, along with other not-so-scientific data that they emphatically support as reality.

I believe I'm easy to deal with and I make friends with virtually anybody, but I have made it a point not to start a close association with superstitious salespeople. Their "disease" may be contagious. I have seen an exceptional case where their influence was so evil and so thorough that a whole sales team became "infected". The whole team was quickly replaced or the company would not have survived the malignancy!

A co-worker once told me that it is easy to spot this breed of salesman. They are the ones that talk too much on meetings usually going on and on over rules and regulations. They dwell exceedingly on exceptions rather than the rules, by taking sides against the company, mostly in situations where they don't have enough information to judge that the company is at fault. They have an answer for everything, and whoever dares to disagree is going to be involved in an argument with no end in sight. I never could prove this theory, but I agree that most of the complainers I met fit almost perfectly in this category, with another thing in common: their production is usually well below average.

In show business (as in sales) not one day is an uneventful day

Not one day in anyone's life is an uneventful day. No day is without profound meaning, no matter how dull and boring it might seem. It doesn't matter whether you are a seamstress or a queen, a shoeshine boy or a movie star, a renowned philosopher or a Down's syndrome child. In every day of your life there are opportunities to touch someone's life.

Some people joke that a salesman (or anybody on commission for that matter) wakes up every morning unemployed. Independent of his past sales record, he needs to create some new business or his sales career is finished. That is the only thing our working days have in common.

For a salesman, each day should be fulfilling. On one side we are providing for ourselves by closing a deal, on the other hand we had our client's needs understood and satisfied. We are now (for better or for worse) part of their life experience. To make these contacts beneficial for both parties is what brings fulfillment to those involved. It is the mystical side of our careers that I specially treasure.

Considering that we are selling every time we interact with other human beings, it is our obligation to make these associations as constructive as we can. Little acts of kindness can go a long way. It will work with our clients, our family, our co-workers, and anybody else we happen to network with.

In sales, as on stage, each day is full of opportunities, open to improvements and ready to become unforgettable. And who decides how each day goes? Each one of us – and I wouldn't want it any other way!

Good actors begin with the end in mind

Almost all of the world-class athletes and other peak performers are visionaries. They see it, feel it; and experience it before they actually do it. They begin with the end in mind. You can do it in every area of your life. Before performance, a sales presentation, a difficult confrontation, or the daily challenge of meeting a goal, see it clearly, vividly, and relentlessly... over and over again. Create an internal "comfort zone" for each uncomfortable situation. When you get into those circumstances they won't scare you, they aren't foreign.

The same is true for the expectations we have in the sales world. Going to a sales presentation visualizing that is going to be a failure, makes this encounter just that: a failure. An interesting quote, that I would give credit to the authors if I could remember who they are, mentions this truth: "If you think you can or if you think you can't – you're right!"

It's not only a question of positive thinking making things happen. A home is supposed to reflect its blueprint. If the blue print defined six windows, we shouldn't expect three or four. We created the blue print and the real product (the house) should look just like it.

To dwell on the fact that we may lose a sale is to block ourselves to the possibility of closing it. We won't be aware of the opportunities that usually come up, and the results will be a representation of what we anticipated. We did ourselves a disservice and unfortunately deserve the consequences.

Discover what the subtext (in the script) is and use it to your advantage

Subtext is, obviously, what you really mean under what you say. When you say, "I'm going to bed" sometimes what you really mean is "I don't want to talk to you." As a sales professional I've found that is imperative to find out what is the subtext in each part of the presentation. Knowing the intention behind the script gives me power to direct my client to think (and act) in a way that will conduct to a stimulating negotiation.

Attaining a full understanding of the subtext has other advantages.

First, you will be able to present a more in-depth performance.

Second, if you forget a line you can more easily ad lib.

Third, if the client changes subjects and goes on in unrelated conversation (yes, this sort of thing happens all the time) you can get back on track with less noticeable stumbling about.

Asking to myself what the subtext is can improve my work more immediately than almost any other tool. It's interesting that when I identify the subtext, I also define the course of action to be taken. The same is true when we try to decode our clients' unspoken intentions, which can unlock a confronting situation, and a disturbing scene. Our job should be twofold: uncover the subtext in our message, as well as get busy decoding the client's conversation. This approach will deeply influence the way we relate to each other. If the scene (presentation) is eluding you, concentrate on the subtext for the other character as well as your own, and see if the communication isn't wonderfully improved.

Becoming the master of our craft

Few people outside our trade can even begin to appreciate the amount of work and time it takes to develop into an above average salesman. Not a personality. Not a type. Not a specific profile, which can be duplicated, but a master of his craft.

By master of the craft, I mean the master of a technique (or combination of techniques) that you can rely upon deal after deal in any and all situations.

Not many people are ready to invest that much time and effort in their sales career. The emphasis usually is not on career development, but on quick returns. And anybody in sales can name a number of professionals who left the sales business for something less profitable because the "price to pay for success was too high".

Initial frustration is part of the process and it can't be avoided. There is no concert pianist alive who hasn't spent years practicing scales. There is no winning athlete who hasn't come back from a few bad games. There is no top salesman that hasn't overcome disappointment, fatigue or financial stress in order to get to that higher degree of excellence. The good side is that the frustrations are soon forgotten and the laurels remain to remind us that it was a long, but worthwhile journey, although with no destination in sight.

Muhammad Ali said: "It's lack of faith that makes people afraid of meeting challenges, and I believe in myself." Many people never pursue their dreams, not because they don't have dreams or because they don't know how to get there, but because they don't have the faith in themselves to be able to carry out their dreams. We can sometimes look at successful people, especially the very successful, and believe that they are somehow better than us or different than us. We believe in them, but not in us. Most successful men and women in the world are not much different than you and me. I wonder how many boxers could have been another Muhammad Ali but didn't believe enough in themselves to get there.

There is a limited number of seats in the building... don't oversell tickets

It is well known that "there is not such a thing as too much of a good thing". Maybe is with this is mind that salespeople run around (often in circles) trying to meet as many clients as they can. They want to do it all in the least amount of time, which sacrifices the quality of their presentations and stresses themselves beyond their limits. If they would only analyze the results they would see that it usually doesn't turn out to their advantage.

How many salespeople overload their agenda with more than they can handle? Probably, because they were told that success in sales is a numbers game. The inevitable consequence is that while talking to one client his mind is actually on the next client, which is unfair to both, and usually a disaster for the salesman's career.

If turning away potential business sounds like a bad idea, then consider pre-qualifying your clients so you plan to see first those with fit the profile of the majority of your best clients, either in financial status, credit worthiness, place of residence, or other measurement specific to your field of action.

In show business, there are a limited number of seats in the theater. In order to reach a larger audience, it's necessary to consider other venues: more show times, longer season, or taking the show on the road. What can't be done is to sacrifice the quality of the performance, in hopes to cash in the box office. On the long run, it never worked, and it never will.

Always serve the author's (sales manager) intention

There is always a reason behind a script as there is a reason behind a sales presentation. They exist primarily so we don't "reinvent" the wheel at every encounter with a customer. It does sound easier to cut corners and to jump over some parts that may not seem important. The result however is, more likely than not, a disaster.

Unless we own our own business and fully assume the risk, it's not our business to change the management's intention with that script. If the goal is to get the customer to choose your company over a competitor, changing the script will defeat the purpose. Actually, even business owners know that it is in their best interest fight the temptation of making any changes to a script that is fulfilling its purpose – to increase sales!

Identify the main intention behind your scripts and focus on it. Nobody ever got hurt doing that, but many left successful careers because they wouldn't abide by this important guideline. Control your urge to deviate from the main line of thought as defined by the script. Salespeople may justify that "the customer didn't need the whole message". This line of thought may sound fine, but it is not always true. To get a customer for life, we need to give them a fair opportunity to listen to the message, beginning to end, so they can make an informed decision. Let the customer (and the track record of said script) be the judge.

It is imperative for a director (manager) to know all the elements of movie making (selling)

I know a few salespeople who were very successful, but became a disaster when they were promoted to sales manager. In their minds being a manager is an "offstage" position. They will check on everybody, give their pep talks, motivate the team and pray for the best. Not so... Unless he is out there, as one of the team, selling, negotiating, fighting for a deal, they will lose their touch with reality and won't be of any help.

The reality is that our clientele, in general, is highly sophisticated and getting better every day. These clients – just like us – take advantage of tactics, which may present an obstacle to a close. Being out in the market helps the sales manager to create methods to overcome them. The most common tactics (or excuses) include:

Nibble – After deciding on the purchase, the buyer adds, "Oh, by the way, there is no shipping in large orders like that, right?"

Offended Soul – To minimize the pressure of the message, the client answers, "Oh my goodness, are you serious?"

Good Guy/Bad Guy – During the negotiation you hear "I think it is a really good product, but my partner (spouse, boss, etc) won't even hear of it."

Offer Withdrawn – The client is ok, and because of a small disagreement concludes "This is ridiculous, forget the whole thing."

Immediate Deadline – An immediate deadline can put some "pressure". For instance, "If I don't close soon, I'll have my budget transferred to another project."

Higher Authority – We all heard the famous: "Well, this all looks pretty good, but I'll need to check with my partner (spouse, etc), unless we can change the terms to meet my expectations."

Very few companies ask their managers to be salespeople as a sidekick job, or to go out with the sales force once in a while, but the ones that have done it know how wise it proved to be. The manager can discuss the frustrations of his workers because he has "been there, done that", literally. It can be of greater benefit to the group if he listens to the market, first hand, and know the changes, the demands and the opportunities out there.

Successful actors don't need to be arrogant

Successful actors, as well as salespeople can in all justice be proud without being arrogant. It takes pride to win the day. It takes pride to build towards our rightful ambition. It takes pride in consistent accomplishment. But the key to becoming a good leader is being proud without being arrogant.

I believe the worst kind of arrogance is arrogance resulting from ignorance. It's when you don't know that you don't know. Now that kind of arrogance is intolerable. If someone is smart and arrogant, we can somewhat tolerate that. But if someone is ignorant and arrogant, that's just too much to take.

On the same token, we need to learn to be strong but not rude. It is an extra step you must take to become a powerful, capable leader with a wide range of reach. Some people mistake rudeness for strength. It's not even a good substitute.

Good salespeople also learn to be kind, but never weak. We must not mistake kindness for weakness. Kindness isn't weak. Kindness is actually a certain type of strength. We must be kind enough to tell somebody the truth, in a constructive way. We must be kind enough and considerate enough to lay it on the line. We must be kind enough to tell it like it is and not deal in delusion.

When interacting with our clients or colleagues, we must be bold but not a bully. It takes boldness to build our influence, and we've got to walk in front of our group. We've got to be willing to take the first arrow, tackle the first problem, and discover the first sign of trouble.

A top producer is humble, but not timid. Nobody can get to the high life by being timid. Some people mistake timidity for humility. Humility is almost a God-like word; a sense of awe; a sense of wonder – an awareness of the human soul and spirit! Humility understands the distance between us and the stars, and yet has the certainty that we can reach for the stars!

In summation, humility is a virtue, and timidity a disease, an affliction. Timidity can be cured, but it may become a major obstacle to success in sales.

Attitude is like crayons… You can color any moment with them

Attitude is everything… Somewhat unoriginal, but very true! Our worst moments in life can be made bearable with the right attitude. In sales, the ups and downs, the rejections as well as the confrontations, the long days, or phases of meager commissions, are all part of the large picture.

I don't have any scientific proof, but I do believe that the right attitude can be developed by virtually anyone. It's a question of discipline, at first, and then, after enjoying the benefits we start acting in a positive manner because of the rush of energy that it gives us. It creates sparkle to go through a situation, otherwise unpleasant to deal with. It's at the same time a weapon and a shield. However, developing the right attitude seems to be difficult for most people in the sales industry.

The high-quality professionals are self-conscious and are always watching themselves for those short bursts of gloominess. At the first sign of dullness, they take action. Most use daily affirmations to reverse desolation and sense of failure.

Affirmations should be simple, direct and only works in homeopathic dosages, i.e. a little every day, for as long as possible. After a while it becomes engrained on our daily behavior, and we routinely show it as part of our daily life.

It is as exciting to deal with a salesman with the right attitude, as it is depressing to deal with someone with a depressing mood. The clients act the same way and will be attracted by those with a positive approach to their job, their message and their personal life. They will also resist to salespeople who don't seem excited about what they do, and they will take the proper action: ignore the message, and fight back the messenger.

Turning your sales career into a successful venture starts with a positive attitude. Develop a passion for what you are doing. Within the past 24 hours how many positive thoughts have you enjoyed? How often do you reflect on all the positive things you've done with your life? If your answers to these questions disappoint you, it's time for a change.

We all heard that success is not a destination – but a journey. Get your ticket, and enjoy the ride. Your positive outlook towards life will directly influence you success in business. Do you think it's time to fine-tune your attitude?

Plan your future and dare to dream

Do you have a dream that you just can't get yourself to believe that it can become a reality? Then, perhaps you need to get a plan to achieve that dream! If you don't believe it, it is probably because you can't conceive how it will happen. When you plan it out, the dream becomes achievable in your mind! And if you believe it, truly believe it, deep down in your heart, nothing will prevent you from achieving it!

You may not be able to pursue your dream right now. Maybe you are in a time of learning skills or building a career. Actors, like salespeople, know that there is a lot of waiting time prior to glory. Perhaps you are working hard on your job so you can save the money to finance your dreams. That's okay - there is a time for everything.

Whatever happens, don't let your dreams die while you are waiting. Keep them alive! In fact, reserve a room in your heart for them. Sneak down and feed them regularly. Let them grow so when you let them out they are vibrant and strong! They may be waiting now, but they will charge forth to their freedom someday. Like some people, don't give up and let your dreams die.

Our goals (or dreams) are in reality a treasure. We should check on them frequently to make sure we are in the right course of action to reach them sometime soon. Review them very regularly. At least three times a week is what I would recommend. Think little goals and you can expect little achievement. Think big goals and you'll win big success. The first ingredient for your success is to dream a great dream.

The main point would be to have your goals, and if possible the specific plan to achieve them, all written down. If you have not done it yet, get to it. If you do, print them out where you can get to them on a regular basis. This will program your mind to focus in on these priorities of yours and you will function more along the lines that you want to. Your behavior will soon be affected by the dreams you have, they will influence your daily decisions. Take some time today to figure out your goals. Now write them down. Put them in a spot where you will be able to review them regularly. Enjoy your growth towards the hall of fame!

Everybody can be a teacher; the secret is to be willing to learn as much as you can

You can learn from other people to make up for your lack of experience in any area of life. Be open and receptive to people around you. They have things to teach you. Take advantage of the people that have made the journey ahead of you.

A word of caution: Try to pick the right role models. Don't look for people that make you feel good or entertain you. Look for people that can actually help. Role models are more than people you like and admire.

The key is to look for people that will help you be more successful. You can learn different approaches to overcoming challenges. You can learn from the mistakes of others. Learning what not to do is as important as learning what to do.

I believe we can learn the most from ordinary people with extraordinary personality, skills, achievements or purpose in life.

A recent study found that salespeople admire those in authority because of a few specific traits:

Honesty – Being worthy of trust.

Competency – Being capable and effective.

Vision – Sense of direction and concern for the future.

Ability to inspire – A person's capacity to communicate in ways that encourage other people to improve their own behavior.

If we truly want to achieve balanced success in this life, we would be well off finding people who are truly deserving of our admiration. As we admire them, we can have our lives shaped by their influence, a powerful force in guiding us to be what we long to become. Find someone today who you haven't necessarily admired in the past. Think about those things in his life that are admirable. Then decide to work on those things in your own life. And if you want to double your blessing tell that person, in a very direct way, what exactly you admire about them!

If you miss the values, you have missed it all

Values are the things that we believe in and which we think are important. Each person has a value system, which has been influenced by their background and their philosophy of life.

Contrary to what some may think, values do matter to a successful salesman – their values are indeed at the heart of everything they do. Our inner values ultimately determine who we are and who we will become. It is a good idea to prioritize our values in such a way that when they conflict with one another we will have a pre-established idea of which ones we don't dare to discard.

Some jobs respect our personal standards, while other occupations go against certain values we consider non-negotiable. You should clearly notice that a job that supports your value system would interest and motivate you far more than a job that goes against it.

Because there is a strong relationship between jobs and lifestyle, the things that you value in your lifestyle - income, location, free time, etc. - can also play an important part in your career choice.

Sometimes we resist doing what we know is right. I don't want to get into moral definitions of right and wrong, but we all have a very good idea of what is ethical. If we don't, the craving to reach a win-win situation with our client is my best definition of a positive, fundamental, value.

When someone does the wrong thing knowing it is wrong, two things may be happening: Either they haven't developed the habit of neutralizing strong inner urges that tempt them; or they have established the wrong habits and don't know how to eliminate them effectively.

Your audience is free to choose where they go

As rude as it may be, anybody in the audience can stand up and leave the theater at anytime, if they feel inclined to do so. In the sales business our clients know that they can choose either our competitors or us. It is the way we care for our customer that can nullify all our competitor's efforts. I would point four tips on the proper care of your customers.

Feed them with attention. Show them you care. Feed them information about you company, your new products, the market place, and any other information that can help in their decision. Even when they are already your client doesn't mean they know everything going on in your business. If you won an award, expanded your business, delivered a new product or service, let them know. This shows them that you are not stagnating and will continue to be there for them in the future.

Don't let your customers get choked by problems. If there's a problem with your product or service that is affecting your customer, do everything possible to resolve it. The best way to know if there are problems is to ask. Don't wait for your customers to call you with problems. Call them and ask how things are going and be prepared to jump to the rescue if there are problems. We all know someone who pays a little more, or travels a little further to deal with a business simply because they like the relationship and the support. It isn't always about money, but it's almost always about the relationship. Keep the bugs, and competitors, away.

Prevent wild growth of your customer base. Salespeople need to prune their customers or else they will grow larger than their capacity to service their clients successfully. Don't be afraid to walk away from business. Don't be afraid to fire your customers. If they are causing you to move into a direction that is not the focus of your business or that is not in line with your business plan, tell them what you think, so they can either work within your business strategy or move on to another vendor. Controlled grow is good growth!

Follow up consistently. There is a lot that needs to be done to ensure healthy plants. This means you have to care for them and care about them. The same is true with your clients. In addition to the previous tips, general caring is in order. Stay in touch and don't be a stranger.

You sold them your product; therefore, it is your responsibility to make sure it is indeed what they needed, that it solved the problem in which it was intended, and that they know you honestly care about their personal growth and success. Caring means going beyond a client-vendor relationship. It's about a partnership. You take care of them, and they'll take care of you – year after year. This is more cost-effective and efficient for you, and better for your clients since they continue to benefit from what you have to offer and from your lifetime relationship.

Dealing with the working conditions

Both selling and acting equally demand patience and total commitment. While under a self-employment contract, salespeople are frequently required to work long hours and travel. Evening work is a regular part of both professional's lives. Flawless performances require tedious memorizing of lines and repetitive rehearsals.

A successful professional need stamina to withstand the usual professional attire, the long, irregular hours, and the adverse weather conditions that may exist "on location". In some cases, traveling is necessary. Salespeople often face the anxiety of intermittent alternation of sales and non-sales appointments, as well as rejections when presenting their products, sales or services.

Some people put unnecessary emphasis on the negative aspects of our jobs. It has been an obstacle to some people when they consider a career in sales. Most don't recognize that there is a lot of freedom hidden underneath the otherwise miserable working conditions. Good planning, on the salesman's part, may result in flexible schedule. Long trips may be combined with short but memorable sightseeing. A few rejections may become a driving force leading us to improve our presentations, our effectiveness and, as a natural result, our income.

Of course, working conditions are affected by two main variables: the company policies and the salesman status within the company. Some companies do have strict rules that may seem hard to follow.

I have found, from experience, that most, if not all of those strict rules, are negotiable, when the salesman performs above average. It's a given. The company wants production and they are willing to compromise, rather than lose a top producer. However, taking advantage of every exception destroys the image that one should have of professionalism and respect to company policies. Make use the exceptions, but don't open the door for conflicts and damaged relationship with co-workers and managers.

Likewise, managers (directors and producers), contrary to what salespeople think, often work under stress as they try to meet schedules, stay within budgets, and resolve personnel problems while putting together an acceptable production.

What is in it for me?

Base salary (which is not the norm in sales), working hours, commission structure and other conditions of employment are covered by self-employment laws, and are usually discussed between management and salespeople during the recruiting and training process. These initial interviews and pre-hiring training are a perfect time to ask questions, without going too deep into hypothetical situations.

The Actors' Equity Association, the Screen Extras Guild and the American Federation of Television and Radio Artists represent actors. Similarly, the salesman can count on specific laws (and associations) that were created to protect him. It's our responsibility to learn about productivity bonus, commission draws, covered expenses (mileage, accommodation, etc.), as well as discounts (or possible deductions) from the gross commission.

Working long hours, in most professions, is the key for a higher income. In sales, however, we have yet another way to increase our earnings. For example, selling more to each customer may boost our commissions, without necessarily taking more working hours. It's a benefit often overlooked, but available, nonetheless. If working long hours is a by-product of our career, increasing the purchase power of our clients will become a source of freedom and of higher financial benefits.

Usually taxes are solely the salesman's responsibility. It may, however, be another financial hazard if not addressed properly. Making sure that our taxes, fees, association dues, and others, are paid on time will avoid future disasters, some of them extremely destructive.

It's very common, as we compare professions, to establish that salespeople have one of the highest paying jobs out there. It may seem simple to work in sales, considering that the guidelines are somewhat lose and no specific educational background is necessary in most areas. However, it becomes a very stressful career, with a very hectic schedule, an extremely competitive market and a dramatically bad image from the client's point of view.

Sales Managers experience a different range of income. They usually have a base salary plus commission. The fixed amount varies based on his experience, the size of the selling team and the company size and profitability. The commission is the motivation to get him to maintain sales at the highest possible level.

An actor should never make assumptions about the audience

A very common mistake both for an actor and a salesman is to pass swift judgments and base his behavior entirely on that. Many salespeople have missed sales by believing that the client looks too poor, too unsophisticated, too knowledgeable, too dumb, too antagonistic, or any other things that later proved to be totally wrong and harmful to the success of the sale.

Clients usually expect you to come in, present your play (demonstration) and go. They are not expecting you to be interested in their personal lives, their achievements, and their family goals. That's where a good actor surprises the audience and gets them off guard. If anything could be said about the spontaneous conversation that should start any first contact, it is that a good ice-breaking period can open the doors to a smooth sales presentation, more than virtually anything else we could do.

Experienced salespeople take as much time as it's needed during the ice-breaking period, hoping to create a foundation that will encourage the customer to listen, follow the presentation's flow and hopefully buy the product. Plus, you actually know the client, and you don't need to second guess their reaction, or assume details of his personality incorrectly. We can't force the audience to react according to our expectations. Be ready for surprises. If a salesman insists in pre-judging their clients he will find out they are wrong more often than not.

Avoid trying to show the audience what you want them to feel. Let them express their feelings and work on those feelings according to the client's perception of them. Try hard not to pre-define the result. No matter how it seems, give your client a chance to show interest in their own personal way, and get surprised with higher success rates.

An actor (a salesman) must learn the words of the script (presentation) and work it with emotion

Salespeople, as well as actors, affect the audience with emotions, not conversations. And in both professions one thing is fundamental: one presentation is NEVER comparable to another. Take in consideration that acting (selling) is not about talking but about behaving.

The clients are obviously different, but most important, the salesman will stress one point above the other in different presentations, some points will take longer to get across, and others will be brief, due to lack of interest or due the client's specific needs. All salesmen should use this common advice to actors: Don't act (sell) without feeling (emotion)! Stir the audience, let them realize what you're saying is true.

The secret is to react according to the emotion and objective of the script (presentation). Who said that following a script is boring? Bring your feelings (emotions) to the presentation and cause a power surge that will move the audience into full participation.

Every moment in the sales demonstration is nothing more than story telling… Find out what's the story (script of the presentation) then stay consistent with it. Go through it each time as if it was the first time. For a good performer (salesman) every moment can be different and exciting. Make each presentation the very best, and be ready to enjoy the positive results.

Actors should always be relaxed even through emotional moments. Whatever you do, stay loose. Work on the clientele heartstring… Audience is sentimental. Remember that emotions, not your ideas, move the audience.

Shape up yourself as well as your performance

With few exceptions, sickly people do not become successful salespeople. We know of painters and composers who wrote or painted masterpieces while handicapped. For the salesman however, the road is the battlefield. You have to be there, energetic, excited, and motivated.

Of course health is such an individual matter. Some of us need more sleep, some don't. Diet however is fundamental to most people, to the point that a few companies give some additional training to their employees regarding their nutritional needs. As far as smoking and alcohol is concerned, their use and the quantity is a personal decision and, as long as it doesn't affect someone's stamina, I leave it unmentioned.

Indiscriminate usage of prescription drugs has been a problem with some people I worked with, and the bad news is that they knew the undesirable side effects did not justify their use. I never saw the benefit of it. Coincidently all those people are now in low-paying jobs outside of sales, which came to show that drugs (legal or illegal) have no place in a sales oriented company.

Again, I feel very strong about drugs of any kind. I don't believe that anyone needs them in order to produce. As far as getting "turned on", I can only say this: I wish that their work would "turn them on"; that the excitement and the thrill and the responsibility of being a top producer would sustain them past and beyond what any artificial method would do.

Paraphrasing from the movies, salespeople are supposed to be a "lean, mean, selling machine." With all the pressures on a salesman's shoulders, it's common to wonder how we deal with fatigue and insomnia. The only possible answer: discipline! The best way to deal with fatigue is to avoid it – that is, to be in such peak physical condition that your endurance is never overtaxed. Sometimes, of course, we can be extended beyond our normal powers. Here is where strength of mind is important. We force ourselves to stay in control of the situation. We force ourselves to stay alert and concentrate.

Inspiration vs. Perspiration

There are two paths to the stage of a great theater company: The paths of INSPIRATION and PERSPIRATION.

The actors who are so wonderful, so charismatic, and so powerful on stage that they don't have to do much to get cast best represent inspiration.

The actors who wouldn't be able to do anything without a major company behind them represent perspiration. Take away the super-budget, the mega-publicity, the spotlights of Oscars and other awards, and nothing else is left. Talent is missing, self-discipline is lacking, and power to convince the audience is non-existent.

In sales, as someone once said, 95% is perspiration and 5% is inspiration. It might as well, because self-discipline, talent and consistent practice generate powerful results. The bottom line is that the measure for success is always determined by the result. As simplistic as it seems, that's the way we keep score in the sales world, and the charted result becomes the measuring unit for success.

I don't deny the importance of certain native-born talents. However, regardless of what we've been blessed with at birth, nothing will materialize unless our potential is mobilized and channeled into one direction. At the same time, talent is not an absolute that will resist change and growth. Talent can – and must – be developed. The key is motivation.

In sales there is simply no substitute for motivation. The only way we can possibly go through this long and arduous (but make no mistake... fulfilling) process of becoming a salesman is to *want* or *need* it badly to begin with. There is no way to overstate the amount of hard work, tedium, frustration, and disappointment that fills a sales career. Those who are not strongly motivated simply won't put up with it.

There is no escape. Someone who wants to become a successful salesman must accept the fact that the development process is never-ending. The productive sales person is always striving, always learning, always improving, long after he has established him or herself.

A name, a picture, a slogan, a mission statement

If I asked you to name a few artists based on the following information would you be able to do it?

The personification of Moses…

The old blue eyes…

The guy who gets no respect…

Can you recognize the artists I just described?

As a salesman, who are you? Or better yet… how people describe you? Is there anything (positive!) about you that sticks up when your name is mentioned?

Ask your clients who they think you are. Listen to the answers. Do they know your values, your basic goals, and your professional behavior? Most of the time they don't. In most industries, the competition is fierce and being visible is the key. You need to set a mark… Put yourself in a position above your competition. A few things may help:

Your name: The most basic information to get you known among clients and potential clients.

Your picture: If feasible, let them "see" you before they meet you. It helps them recognize your efforts when they get in contact with other of your marketing efforts.

Your slogan: Make it simple, make it unique, but avoid those simplistic play on words that seem like it was created by a 10 year-old. It should deliver a message, with purpose, hopefully reflecting your objectives and promises.

Your mission: Have it written, share it often, review it once in a while and stick to it.

Those simple steps, if consistent, will present your image in a way that most salespeople won't.

Even if your clients don't share your values, they will respect the fact that you are open about your position, and don't make excuses for being who you are. Use your name, your picture, your slogan and your mission as a way to open doors, and if possible, as a way to keep your image in their minds.

[If you couldn't figure out the answers above, here they are: Charlston Heston, Frank Sinatra, and Rodney Dangerfield.]

Create your character (as a salesman) and give him a life of his own

A certain freedom washes over you when you realize that every day is a day you can create! You don't have to have your day painted for you. You have the power to pick up that brush, choose your colors and begin to make the best of your day (and your life for that matter)! "But my boss makes me sit in an office in front of a computer all day," you may say. Well, you can choose what music you will listen to while working. You can most assuredly choose what attitude you will have. You can choose to leave at lunch or on a break and enjoy whatever activity will bring you joy!

Take responsibility for your life today! Take responsibility for your own attitudes and actions, and for your future. People who will not take responsibility for their lives feel powerless. They feel like they can't achieve their dreams, and this causes them intense feelings of frustration. It is always someone else's fault, or the circumstances are the culprits.

A person's dream can become reality today. At the very least you can begin your journey toward seeing your dreams come true. The first step is taking responsibility. Recognize that you are responsible for making your dreams come true. Your decisions will be the ones that make or break you or your career. Your attitude is the one that will lift you up to heaven or drag you down into the depths. Your actions are the ones that will bring you the fruition of your dreams or leave you longing for something more. Your attitude can, and will, take you in whichever way you choose.

If you are in debt, go get a second job or cut up a credit card. Whatever you need to do to take an action of responsibility today – do it! Understand that you can choose joy and peace by making the decision of what picture to paint. Then pick up that paintbrush and dip into a color you love. Now, with big bold strokes or perhaps fine, small strokes, make of your day what you will. Just remember that the picture doesn't get painted the way you want it until you actually begin to paint!

Visualize the whole play (presentation), but focus on each scene

One of the mistakes of time management is to assume that things will take care of themselves in the long-term. Things never just take care of themselves! Each and every long-term goal we have is strictly determined by each short-term action we take. I have an equation that I use: "Your short-term tasks, multiplied by time, equal your long-term accomplishments." In other words, if you want to save a million dollars, you better save a few each day. If you want to write a 250-page book, write a little each day. If you want to lose 50 pounds, lose a little each day. Little by little, moment-by-moment, stick to your minutes, then your hours, days, weeks, and months, with the assurance that the years will take care of themselves! What is it you want to accomplish long-term? Set up a strategy to get there slowly but surely. Now take the first small step today! Get going and you will experience the joy of your fulfilled destiny!

Do you ever wake up in the morning and think, "I just don't want to get out of bed?" Do you ever feel like quitting in the middle of the afternoon? Of course you do - we all do! The big question is "how do I keep from actually giving up into my lack of motivation?" This is why knowing your purpose is imperative!

Knowing your purpose in life and in your profession, and knowing it with a clarity that borders on brilliance, is the one way to restart an unmotivated heart! When you begin to feel like sitting around, go back to your purpose. If it is clear to you, and if it is a powerful purpose in the first place, your engine will start firing fast again!

Take some time today to put down on paper what your life purpose is. Make it just a few sentences so you can remember it the next time you feel like giving up or being lazy. Make it as clear as you can! If you are feeling unmotivated today, take some time to think through the purpose you have in life.

The ability to keep your purpose in the forefront of your mind, with a high degree of clarity is the sure cure for a lack of motivation.

Separate yourself from the character

Don't show who you (the actor, the salesman) really are. It may antagonize the audience. If you like certain things, don't disclose openly as it may confront the buyer, unnecessarily.

Your character (a successful salesman, remember?) is never a religious fanatic, neither opinionated. By no means extremely liberal or hard-core conservative... Expressing radical points of view may cause your clients to withdraw from a business relationship. Perhaps you will find an opportunity today to become angry. Resist the temptation! Take a step back from the situation and be calm and speak clearly.

Commit to acting, not reacting. Make today a day of calm discussion of the issues, not the bitter shock of personalities. Step back and speak from the strength of your cause. If you have a hard time, excuse yourself until you can regain control and act professionally.

People who are successful take ownership of their lives and refuse to see themselves as victims. How many truly successful people have you have met who sit around whining about how bad things are because the deck is stacked against them? Conversely, how many unsuccessful people have you found like that? Too many to number? We are not captives of our environments but captains of our destiny. You can choose whatever future you desire! Take time today to reflect upon your life. Is the general situation in which you find yourself in less than ideal? If so, determine today to stop whining and start winning! Get off of your inertia and go for it!

Get you mind set on what the character (you as a salesman) really wants

Your character (the salesman) wants the deal. Work towards it. A "no" from a client is almost never the end of the negotiation. Be creative. Brainstorm with the clients what can be done to close the sale, while preserving a win-win situation for both parties.

If the cost is a problem, can we give him some advice on financing? If the credit worthiness is a barrier, can we look for alternate lenders? If one decision maker is not willing to accept the terms, can we carefully listen to his objections and try to address them with logical, possible solutions?

It has been said that a client says "no" to a fair offer only when he doesn't understand some of the terms. Usually, he is not sure of the extent of his commitment, and is afraid that some misunderstood items will turn this deal into a future nightmare (financially or otherwise).

This part in a negotiation is probably the most exciting. A salesman will seldom have two negotiations exactly alike. Some guidelines may help, when faced with objections during the first part of the negotiation process:

- Slow down your normal conversational speech. Use longer pauses between sentences. Give time to the customer to hear and process everything you are saying.
- Be mindful of the customer's objections. Show respect towards those thoughts and never lessen their value.
- Always ask open-ended questions to get down to the real objection (which the client usually expresses non-verbally).
- Confirm that you understand those objections. The best way is to paraphrase them, being careful not to look down on them or sarcastically discard them as foolish.
- Certify that there are no other issues preventing them from agreeing. Answer each objection truthfully and directly.
- Re-estate the offer (with all the changes agreed upon, if any) and ask for their business.

Remember, the salesman may be pressed for time, have other engagements, or be otherwise stressed. But the character you play is there for the sale, and will not give up until every single possibility has been considered. The character mind set is always focused on closing every single sale.

The journey to success involves more than just a few steps

There are several steps you can take to enhance your attitude. Here are some of my own favorites:

Improve your Self-Image. When was the last time you looked at yourself in the mirror? If you weren't happy with what you saw, what can you do to change the picture? What's that? You never look in a mirror? Well, get some mirrors today. Place one in a spot you cannot avoid when you are getting ready for the day; when you see yourself looking your personal best, you will feel better. Place another mirror so you can see yourself when you are talking on the phone and while you are working at your computer. You will be able to see your body language as you are delivering your messages. You will be amazed at the difference it makes in what you say and how you say it.

Listen to Motivational People. Have you ever noticed how quickly being around other positive people and listening to them talk can lift your own spirits, leaving you feeling good about yourself? Surround yourself with positive people as much as you possibly can. Make an effort to communicate with positive people at work and within your community every day. When you can't get out, listen to motivational audiotapes, watch motivational videos, and attend motivational seminars. It's up to you to internalize what you learn from those tapes and seminars and use what you've learned to your advantage.

Talk to the Winner in you! Get rid of all the negative words in your vocabulary. You won't have problems, only *issues* and *challenges*. No more taking risks or chances; from now on, only *adventures* and *opportunities*. Think about what you say and write. If any of it can be construed as negative, find a way to reword it and memorize the new, positive words you've substituted. Accepting *can't, don't* and *won't* as answers to all your challenges may keep you from reaching your goals and from becoming as successful as you can.

Volunteer to help others. Visit your local homeless shelter and volunteer some time. It won't take you long to see just how fortunate you are, plus it's a great way to generate ideas on how to make our country a better place so less fortunate people can enjoy positive experiences, too.

Talk to the principal at your nearest public school and ask if there isn't a way you could volunteer a couple hours. When you spend some time with the future of our country, you will become inspired to forge ahead.

Participate in meaningful programs at your association, union or community. The benefits are twofold (personal growth and direct contact with prospective clients).

Develop your sense of humor. Even if you weren't born a humorist or comedian, you can experience some rather amusing moments in life by being more observant. Scan the headlines of your local paper or read its cartoon section. You're bound to find something amusing in your local paper every day. Watch children at play. They can make you laugh without trying.

Spend quality time with family and friends. It's rare for entrepreneurs to be able to give their family and friends a lot of time, but if you make every minute count, you will feel better about yourself and they will be more supportive.

An actor's (salesman) success is complete when others in the entertainment industry (co-workers) respect him, as well as his work

When other salespeople describe you, what do they say? What words do they use? What are your strongest character traits? What are your values? Are your character traits and values reflected in your daily work and relationships? Are they part of the sales culture you have created within your organization? Are you *modeling* what it takes to be a really successful salesman? Severe, but important questions!

What those in our industry think of us is as vital for our success as what the clients' think of us. Our clients see the character we represent when in their presence. Our co-workers see the actor. They mingle with us enough to see if we are egocentric, manipulative and omnipotent. When celebrities criticize these traits of personality in other public figures it usually destroys that artist's stardom.

When we do our best to be ethical, fair, polite, respectful, etc., our co-workers will be bound to express their pleasure in being associated with us. Similarly, if co-workers can see nothing but faults on a professional, the criticized fellow is bound to experience a miserable life.

I also believe we can change other people by how we talk to them. We can make people better by praising them. It is a simple reality of humanity that it is natural for us to change based on what people tell us. Success will easily come our way once we realize that it is a direct result of our own actions. We shouldn't allow other people's negative speaking to change us in a negative way. It will be our natural tendency to have that opinion become a reality if we listen long enough.

But, good news! It doesn't have to be that way! You can put so much positive stuff into your mind that you will instead become all of that positive reality despite of their negative perception of reality.

Do you have someone who speaks negatively about you? Here are three things you can – and must – do today (and regularly) to overcome that:

One, avoid unnecessary discussions, explanations, or excuses for your behavior, if it seems they are not willing to hear them.

Two, spend some time putting good stuff into your mind.

Three, develop a relationship with someone who will constantly speak nicely to you! If you have someone like that already, take him or her out for lunch or coffee today!

Habit is stronger than reason. Are you controlled by your thoughts, or are you controlling yur thoughts? If you're ruled by your mind you are a king, if by your body, you are a slave.

Accept changes as part of reality

The seasons change, the temperature changes, the sales market changes, the world as a whole changes… why wouldn't our professional reality change? Why are we so afraid of changes? Most of us are afraid of the change itself. Can we survive the change? We love our comfort zone and leaving it is never trouble-free. Life as a performer or as a salesman is no different. We need to change and accept changes in order to enjoy our careers. In some cases we need to accept changes in order to survive!

It is during these unavoidable changing times (in the economy, in the company, in department policies, in management) that we can see a salesman's true colors. The changes become the almighty power, which will either destroy our careers or bring doom to the company as a whole. Very seldom this is the case, but to convince a salesman to see the progress that usually follows change is sometimes too much to ask.

The confusing fact is that commonplace salespeople look for changes in the wrong places. They believe the script should change (be simplified), the pay scale should change (be more generous), and management should change (and he would be the best replacement, of course).

Change replaces boredom, enhances enthusiasm, fuels motivation and triumph over the status quo (a plague that has become a way of life for mediocre performers). Change is always welcome when it is focused on improvement, as it usually does.

By using the power to change, we can at any time decide to alter the course of our lives. No one can take that away from us. We can do what we want to do. We can be who we want to be. We have the power to choose which impulse to follow.

While our character is formed by our circumstances, our desires can shape those same circumstances. The one thing over which we have absolute control is our own thoughts. It is what puts us in a position to control our own destiny. Our greatest power is the power to choose.

Wise salespeople will welcome change, understanding that in general change brings growth.

No matter how wonderful a show (or the whole season) is, it will come to an end

A Chinese proverb wisely observes: DON'T ASSUME TREES GROW TO THE SKY. This cannot happen! Yet some fast-growing companies (and some of us, for that matter) act as though their revenues will keep soaring at exponential rates forever. Salespeople have some kind of gene that prevents them for being realistic, and they think that prosperity moments will last an eternity.

In general, the most experienced they become the more they think they can do it without investing in improving their presentations skills. When sales don't go as well as they had been, instead of reviewing their strengths and weaknesses they point towards outside causes. Usually those causes are inevitable, and the turn of events forces the salesman to dive into a depressive mood, with "poor me" and "why now" as the repetitive comments.

On a salesman's point of view, we could never assume that our sales figures will remain steady. While there are ways to prevent extreme variations of income from month to month, there is no way to avoid them altogether.

If I just work hard on things I can control, the results tend to be leveled, without the income variations so common in commissioned sales. A person can define an acceptable minimum performance and build on that. One appointment with a new client everyday, or a minimum number of prospecting phone calls every morning are some good examples.

Our working hours, however, should never be varying according to our income. I call it the "used car salesman syndrome": when I sell more than average, I take off for a month, without considering that when I come back I will find out that there is nothing in the pipeline.

Another way to avoid ups and downs with wide gap is to plan accordingly: at the most 50% of the income should be considered "usable income", 25% should be saved towards taxes, and another 25% be applied on savings (to cover expenses on the low months, retirement, or any other worthwhile goal).

Succeeding where others would fail can direct an actor to fame and success

The first thing that will contribute to reaching your goal is that you simply want to reach it badly enough. You must learn how to desire something with sufficient intensity to be successful. If you have the desire you have the power to attain success. You can really have anything you want in life if you go after it. But you have to want it. As a drowning soul desires air, as a shipwrecked person craves fresh water, so must you feel that intense, eager, insistent, demanding desire for your success!

Your desire for success must be so strong within you that it becomes the very breath of your life. It must be your first thought when you wake up and your last thought when you go to bed at night. You can have anything you want if you go after it with intensity.

Someone said, "The sweetness of victory is magnified by the effort it took to achieve it." An easy win is still a win, but usually there is less satisfaction in it. If things go our way, and we accidentally reach our objectives without much effort, we still get the trophy and the check but you don't get the memory of the fight.

Working hard for a goal is part of the reward itself. And when victory comes, it is sweeter still. Now the winner has the satisfaction of looking back and knowing that the hard work was well worth and that he earned that moment in the spotlight of fame. He should know that the character was forged by hours of hard work. Yes, he earned it, and it feels darn good!

Is there something that you are HOPING will happen? Don't! Work hard and MAKE it happen! You will feel better in that victory than in the simpler one. Set out a strategy of hard work to reach your goal, and then take one step today!

No wonder the hard to get sales are the ones we remember the most, and the ones we brag about as long as there is someone willing to listen. The easy ones, for some salesman, become sort of a failure in disguise. We sweep them under the carpet and hope that our memory will erase them as time goes by. Better yet, we tend to fight hard to replace them with those sales actually worth talking about.

When focus and diversification work together

Diversification (in a sense, the opposite of "focus") is an important aspect of strategy. You do not want all of your eggs in one basket. Suppose you spend many months or even several years gravitating your business around a particular program or system, and then the company fails or your account gets canceled because of some unforeseen event. Your income can suddenly disappear!

My enthusiasm is higher when I'm in control of as many different projects as I can handle. Prospecting for new clients, setting appointments, returning phone calls, solving impasses, negotiating price and closing a transaction are the ingredients of a full day! The more I have to take care of, the more in control I feel.

We need to understand that our job as a salesman has a well-defined ROI (return on investment). Crossing that line, i.e., wasting time with a lost deal, following up on clients with no potential, using mail and personal deliveries instead of fax, e-mail and conference calls, may prove harmful.

As contradictory as it may seem, we need to focus on efficiency, while diversifying our opportunities. The goal is to accomplish more, without wasting precious time. My personal strategy is to have multiple independent income streams, each one with the potential to grow exponentially, as well as a large number of closings "on the pipe".

2) Demonstration

	Qualification	Presentation	Negotiation
Rehearsal	QR	**PR**	NR
Performance	QP	**PP**	NP
Critique	QC	**PC**	NC

Shortcuts will actually cut you short from your goal, your profits, and your success

To be successful and profitable, you must start using the most effective marketing strategies possible. Less obvious, however, is the fact that you must also stop trying to shortcut your way to profits. It can be the most expensive, destructive and most common mistake made by salespeople.

Some businesses marketing plan consists of an ad, flyer or other device that simply announces the business name, possibly lists a few basic features of the product or service and ends with an address and phone number.

The prospect is now expected to respond to this type of marketing piece by immediately purchasing the product or service.

Unless you are offering an extremely high-demand, hard-to-get product/service (an original Van Gogh painting, Super bowl tickets at half price, etc.) this marketing strategy almost always results in little or no response. This strategy is very much like walking up to a stranger at a party and asking, "Would you marry me?" What do you think the response would be?

Look at the local, small business ads in any newspaper and you will find that competitors usually use the same basic format, same basic message, same basic strategy … If everyone else is doing it, then it must be the right thing to do. Remember your mom's admonition, "If everyone was jumping off a bridge, would you want to jump too?"

We feel safe in the crowd. Safe doing what everyone else is doing. We also assume that if it works for them, it can work equally well for us. This line of thought rarely works because your marketing puzzle is unique to your business and each piece must fit perfectly with all of the other pieces.

In addition, whatever success a competitor may be experiencing can often be from a few of their less obvious or visible marketing methods. Often the highly visible element (ad, flyer, brochure, etc.) is one of the least effective. You end up copying the money losers, rather than developing your own profit winners.

You are the president of your fan club

It's up to the salesman to motivate their fan club. The world already has a terrible image of salespeople. Show (by actions more than words) that you are a step above the general image of sales professionals. The clients haven't stopped looking for that kind of person. Logic tells them that not "everybody" will be unethical. They are searching for the "exception to the rule"! They will be willing to do business with anybody that makes them feel comfortable about the person's work ethics, values and principles.

It may be that some of your clients look upon selling as a four-letter word spelled with seven letters. The image shown in movies and on TV, written about in papers and magazines is anything but favorable. Have you ever read what high school and many college texts say about selling . . . "selling is getting people to buy what they don't want or need for more than they want to pay"? Yes, that's what some of the books say. Many people, not just young people, believe that in order to be good at selling they will be required to do something that at least borders on being unethical. That attitude doesn't make for good work habits neither leads to high sales volume.

Adding each client to the list of fans is the ultimate goal. Get each one sold on you and they will start doing the selling "for you", through referrals, endorsements, or testimonials. Just like any fan club, don't forget that it's your responsibility to keep their "appreciation" for you at the highest level possible. The most common way to accomplish that is to keep in touch with past clients on a regular basis.

Taming the nerves

If you do care about the quality of your performance, and care about getting your lines right; if you do care that everybody can hear you speak; that your performance goes as planned, with the client getting the point of your presentation; and that your performance is skillfully crafted, professionally executed, spontaneous, engaging, exciting and fun for everyone involved... then, trust me, you will be nervous. You will be nervous because... YOU CARE.

The nerves are what happen when your performance matters to you – when you want to do good work. Of course, excessive nerves can get in the way of doing good work. So here are a few tips on how to keep control of your performance and prevent excessive nerves from creeping in.

TIP #1 – Memorize your script as thoroughly as possible.

TIP #2 – Understand your reason to present the message.

TIP #3 – Try to become familiar with every place in which you might be presenting your sales. Plan for small and large areas. Test different ways to handle your forms, material, samples, etc.

TIP #4 – Rehearse, rehearse, rehearse – Rehearse until you can't stand rehearsing... then rehearse some more. Read the script every day. The whole script – until it flows naturally! Know the message inside out, outside in, upside down, downside up, backwards, forwards and standing on your head. Become so familiar with the words that you say parts of the script in your sleep... so familiar that at other gatherings your conversation consists almost entirely of lines from the sales script.

TIP #5 – Think about everything you are supposed to do, say, think and feel during the play (presentation). What line should you be saying when you get there? How are you supposed to be reacting to the client's words and actions...? How do they make you feel? If you keep your mind busy, you won't have any time to think about how nervous you are. You'll be too busy thinking of all the gazillions of things you're supposed to be thinking about. A salesman that is too busy thinking of the job at hand is also too busy to be nervous. Review the little things while putting on make up, adjusting your tie, driving to work, walking to the client's door, and every moment from the time you get ready for a day's work, until the time you get home back from a full day.

TIP #6 – You, as a salesman, are like a character in a play. You did not suddenly, magically appear seconds before your contact with a client. What are you willing to share with your clients about you? You get to decide. If you sell houses, you don't disclose the fact that you are renting your home. If you sell natural products you don't disclose the fact that you eat fast food every single day. Don't deceive the client, but make sure you withhold unnecessary and counter-productive information sometimes.

Working as an actor (and salesman) is actually being an entertainer

In a busy lifestyle as we all experience today, why would someone spend some of their precious time with a salesman, unless they get something in return. As the salespeople keep their undivided attention, the presentation develops into a business relationship. Should the entertainment be weak, the words be meaningless – on "auto-pilot" – the disastrous results may hurt or destroy an otherwise successful selling career.

Acting naturally won't take a salesman anywhere. Naturalism is dull. We need to give the clients (audience) an emotional circus. Every moment should be full. Take an emotion and make it big, without exaggerated effort. Turn your sales presentation into something worth watching. The emotion generated by a powerful sales pitch must be strong, but under control. In the end, it must *not* look like acting.

As a side note, it is important to make it clear that entertainment does not necessarily mean funny. Yes, a sales pitch can be funny, but it doesn't need to. Yes, it can be dramatic, but not necessarily. However, it needs to be emotional, consistent, well-defined, involving, somehow bold, and a little refreshing in the client's mind. Of course, this makes us think of salesmanship (or showmanship) in a new way. When you spend hours with clients, and they tell you how sorry they feel that you are leaving, you know that they have been entertained. The hours went fast, like in a good movie or play.

Acting naturally or forcefully

One simple truth in sales that I learned is that every person is transparent. A client, any client, can sense if we are conveying something we really believe in. If a salesman doesn't mean every word in his "script", the audience will certainly notice. Honesty is always the best policy. In sales, I dare to say it is mandatory. This requires a lot of self-discipline on the part of the salesman, especially to avoid the temptation to stretch the sales pitch and be taken by the spur of the emotion. Honesty in sales is the base for trust, and trust is the foundation of a perfect rapport with the client.

To the whiners who would try to establish the fact that they don't care about their product or service, and they are in this field for the money, I would take my crystal ball and read about their future: they won't survive in this field for too long! We cannot create a trusting atmosphere unless we can see the value of our product or service. Actors, no matter how good they are, couldn't act in a convincing manner if they don't understand the message their character is getting across.

Confidence from the part of the client and will and intelligence from the salesman's side are essential. The communication must be brain-to-brain, not empty words to empty ears. The whole idea is to see how much emotion and inner life salespeople, in their performance, can give their character. Be aware that muscle tension is not necessary when showing emotion. Raising your voice or interrupting the client's conversation – although tempting – is never in the salesman's favor.

Salespeople are supposed to give of themselves totally in order to be as natural and real as they are convincing. In science, some physical signs measure emotion: heart rate and electrical impulses. In sales, emotion is measured by the client's understanding and acceptance. Understanding of the message conveyed by the salesman and acceptance of our terms, which may involve price, quality or company's background.

Timing is everything

In comedy, time is everything. A punch line a little earlier or later than the ideal timing and the joke becomes a waste... a waste of time, of course. Inexperienced actors must stay away from trying to play the whole story (presentation) in each scene (phase of the sale's presentation). Just because the actor knows the end of the play, they don't go around divulging if the "butler did it" right in the first act.

It would defuse the suspense and the reviews would be damaging. Self-control is the key here.

Being in the right place at the right time is not just something for the lucky few but a strategy you can achieve by choice. In the sales world, if you disclose to the other party how far you're willing to go in the negotiation, and how desperate you are for the deal, you already paved the way to disaster.

Timing is particularly important when dealing with goals. Reaching your goals is too important to leave it to chance – create a game plan that makes now the right time to win! A short goal on a highly producing month or vice-versa can take all the emotion out of selling at a high level. It can be said that timing is the single most important factor in achieving success – from mastering a daily schedule to forming a life plan that brings continued personal fulfillment and financial reward.

Audience is usually biased towards the nice guy (trustworthy salespeople) in the play (market)

It's no secret that a client will easily buy from someone he trusts. It's no secret that a trustworthy salesman can capitalize on a client by getting higher sales, strong referrals, minimal amount of complaints, and an open communication. This means that most salespeople out there are trying hard to earn the confidence of their clients. Simple as it means, this is not quite so.

Trust is based on subjective feelings, secret reactions, and immeasurable acceptance from the client. It can't be obtained without the client's permission. A client can't be bought, imposed or even blackmailed into trusting us. I would dare to say that trust couldn't be actually taught. It is a natural reflection of our empathy for the client, and their personal situation.

We surely can make our audience believe the story and its details (i.e. the product and its benefits) are real, but not if first we don't believe it ourselves. A simple truth that has caused many salespeople to stumble, as they have tried to convince their clients of something they didn't take the time to accept as being good for the buyer.

Listening to the customer is as necessary as presenting the product. The best way to listen is not to make our mind blank, but stay objective and stay emotional about the company, the product and the benefits of acquiring it.

A word of caution: In our quest for the customer's trust, no matter how at ease your audience puts you, don't make yourself too comfortable. As harsh as it may sound for some, our purpose is not to have a client as a friend or confidant. He should be our ally, our partner, but never more than that. A casual rapport, no matter how healthy it may seem is detrimental to a long-term, professional relationship.

Actors must convey immediacy to the audience

I wish every salesman prior to meeting a client would mentally repeat this mantra: "Do it right the first time. Second time is not as dramatic." There is a sense of urgency that we need to convey to the client, but we usually forget that the salesman is under the same amount of pressure, if not bigger, to avoid losing the contact.

Some guidelines to add urgency to our message include:

- Address a painful consequence about postponing the purchase of your product.
- Make it a limited quantity, or limit the time to act or the number of bonuses (add scarcity)
- Remind them of their personal situation, need or problem – head on – and what life is like while having that need or problem. Call their attention to the fact that they can solve it with the product or service you represent. Remind them how embarrassing it is to have that situation after they know that it can be solved for them.
- Remind them that the insecurity of the future may affect your product availability, or affordability.

If you don't add some urgency on why they should act now, they might say, "Oh, I'll just buy it next pay day." Then they forget or they can't find your site ever again. They should buy NOW, not tomorrow, not next week. Now!

Independently of the product, and with very few exceptions, the client usually makes his decision to buy or not right at the first contact. It's up to us to convey to him or her that this is also our expectation and that it's not a sign of weakness on their part. After all, it's not salesman versus client in one round, as many may think. We are partners. Our job is to present the facts and give them the chance to make the right decision.

I could quote statistics, but I prefer to present basic common-sense facts. The more personal contacts we have with a client, without impressing on him the need for a commitment on his part, the least chance to a firm sale we will have. Multiple encounters, days apart from one another, imply that there is no consensus. It takes a while to build the emotion once it's gone, and we will find ourselves running the first yard over and over again, and never crossing the goal line.

A good play (presentation) has a flow that should lead the audience to a climax and a sense of awe

As creative as an actor may think he is, he shouldn't mix scenes from one part of the play with scenes from another. It would confuse the other actors, the audience, and put at risk the story as a whole. Why, then, salespeople try to run through their script, like a train with no breaks, showing no respect to their clients? Be aware of the key lines and don't miss them. Keep the lines fluid until each pause. It's imperative to use pauses; to create moments of silence; to let the clients speak their minds; otherwise you bother the audience.

At the same time, be ready to ad lib. What can be changed in the scene to better touch the audience?

When things are working for you (as a salesman), don't do anything stupid. The hardest thing for an artist (salesman) is to know when to slow down or even stop. Bad actors may know all the words in the script, but say them in the same rhythm. Lifeless words.

Don't act (sell) with voice only, but use your whole body. Audience needs to be trained. Tell them the main point; avoid the clichés, unless they are part of the script. Don't make repetitive moves, never repeat yourself unnecessarily. It comes naturally, with some practice. As someone once said: "practice by itself doesn't help; perfect practicing is what makes it perfect". There is always room for improvement, go find it...

The audience paid to see the character, and not the actor

It's well known that we all like to talk about ourselves. It is not such a problem, unless we are a salesman where our job is to listen to our clients talk about themselves (and they love to do so)! The clients may seem interested in our lives, but we should offer them only that part that relates to the negotiation moment, never more. It takes some self-discipline (especially for the salespeople with an overfed ego), but it's extremely vital to the sales process. Any exaggeration on our part and we may leave the place with a new friend, but no sales.

To impose ourselves as a professional we may mention our achievements in a very subtle manner. In contrast, to vividly describe oneself as a wonderful person, a loving father, a successful closer might actually intimidate the buyer. Under intimidation, obviously, they will retract and hold important information, which otherwise would help us in defining how to find and meet their needs.

Selling ourselves instead of the product we represent is a common trap, possibly because salespeople are usually brainwashed to sound and look professional, successful and self-assured.

The secret is to look professional, successful and self-assured, but not verbally brag about it. Our performance and personal grooming will send the message across, in a more powerful, believable way. Let's save our words for the sale itself. Having a customer impressed with our self-portrait and lose the sale is bad business.

Action is central to the play (sales)

Action is what you want the other person onstage to do, to feel or to understand. If you are alone onstage, the same definition applies to you. Many books have been written about action in theater. Some theorized that action is the central point of show business. I guarantee that it is central to the sales business! Every actor claims to use it. Salespeople won't go too far without action.

It is obvious that a long presentation comprises hundreds of actions, but very few salespeople will do all the homework. This moment isn't working – what's the action? This objection is unique – what's the action? For an action to get the expected result, it needs to be built upon the counter-balancing obstacle (or objection, or reaction).

The final objective usually is "I want the client to sign the contract". We should then focus so we reach that point, as expected. No action, however, is set in stone. We can try it and, if necessary, modify it. The action shouldn't be a "result", but an attempt. Just try it.

A key building block of performance (and sales) is the balance between action and obstacle. We know that action is what we want the other person to do, but there are obstacles that prevent us to do it effortlessly. Sometimes we either ignore or get intimidated by the obstacle (objection), and if that's the case none of these approaches will solve the situation. A little effort on our part and we could recognize the real objection. Unless we can define the actual objection, we won't be able to plan tactics to overcome it.

Give enough value to the balance between objection and action. If the action is significantly stronger than the objection, the objective is reached too quickly, and the client doesn't value it. If, on the other hand, the obstacle seems too powerful, the action is too soon overpowered and the result is less than acceptable. It's necessary to find the crucial beat.

Convey the right weight to the obstacle, so we can apply the exact power to the action. Remember, your audience wants to pay to see you lift a piano, not a Kleenex. Let him believe that they have put a good fight. Grant yourself the winning point, though. A good turn around of events usually means a lot – in the clients' eyes – towards the clients desire to comply with your request and close the deal.

Getting the process down to a science!

Guessing at the elements of your marketing strategy is probably the worst way to invest your marketing budget. You are practically guaranteeing the same results you would achieve by guessing at the specific sequence of numbers needed to open a combination lock. Since each consecutive step is linked to the success of the previous step, one wrong guess destroys your chances for success.

Most people, including many small business owners, mistakenly believe that marketing is more of an art than a science. Those of the "marketing is art" point of view believe that anyone's opinion concerning marketing is just as valid as anyone else's. In reality, marketing is very much a science with specific principles, rules and quantifiable results. Because of this "marketing is art" philosophy most of what people believe about marketing is based on myths, not facts.

Show some people two ads and ask them to select the one they think is the better ad. Most will select the profit loser rather than the profit winner. Why? Because they are unaware of the bigger picture, and don't recognize the marketing principles and strategies that make a powerful marketing piece a profit winner.

So they base their opinion on such vague, subjective criteria as cleverness, cuteness, different and artistic look, and the ads fun or pun appeal. These criteria rarely have anything to do with generating maximum response but they have everything to do with wasting your marketing investment and destroying your potential sales.

The best way to develop a successful and profitable marketing strategy is to use the knowledge, experience and skills of someone who has already discovered the marketing approaches that do work as well as the approaches that don't work.

These discoveries should always be based on measurable results from objective tests… never subjective opinions or assumptions.

Explore the people. Use things that become a bonding factor with the audience

Any two people can always find something they have in common. Capitalize on any and every interest you might share with your client. The only way to find these recognizable items is to probe the client. Ask them about their family, personal interests, workplace, or background. Let them decide which of those areas they are more comfortable talking about, and just add fuel to the conversation, as needed.

Contrary to what some people may think, asking questions is never offensive. What offends people is to assume without asking. Asking appropriate questions will avoid a common pitfall in sales: the craving we sometimes have to assume things (and suffer the embarrassment of being totally off in our suppositions). Guessing wrong may cost us a sale, some of our income or the dissatisfaction of our client.

A good ice-breaking moment is priceless. And sometimes it only happens once or twice during the whole presentation. It is usually during the initial "courting" time that the client shows or lets down his barriers. It is the foundation of what it is to come (our interaction), and it does define how easy or how hard the sales process will be.

Although every phase of the sale is important, I tend to give more weigh to the ice-breaking part. As the name implies, breaking the ice will provide for a better ride towards our main goal: make the sale and obtain the client's satisfaction.

The audience expects (and in some sense demands) feedback from the artist (salesman)

When people express themselves verbally, they want feedback that they've been heard, and they certainly want to be understood. This is true even when they don't understand themselves, as is the case when a person is uneasy and tries to describe their feelings and thoughts. In most cases, they mumble a few confusing words and – mostly illogical – objections. If we take the time to slow down, and get pass the words, to the real concern, we will most likely win the client's respect and establish a healthy rapport.

If two or more people want to be heard and understood at the same time, and no one is willing to listen, either an argument or a cold-shoulder is almost inevitable. For this reason, a masterful communicator makes his goal to listen and understand first, before attempting to be heard or understood.

In the communication process, each involved party is 100% responsible for conveying the message. As salespeople, our bread-and-butter is at stake every time we meet with a potential buyer. It becomes imperative that we take the time to listen, and visibly show that we care about the client's feelings, reservations or fears. They expect us to openly discuss how he can harmonize those thoughts with the upcoming purchase. Matching their feelings with the benefits of our product or service should be the utmost objective.

Our feedback should involve two main points:

(1) Empathizing, rather than sympathizing

Empathizing means to understand the client's feelings, but not necessarily agree with them, or feel them with the same intensity. Sympathizing means to understand their feelings and try to undergo the same emotions as the client's. Goes without saying, sympathy is not going to lead to a closing, and it's quite damaging for the salesman's emotional stability.

(2) Show clearly that we are listening.

In order to show to our clients that we are listening, it becomes necessary to react, verbally or through body language. Body language is a form of nonverbal communication, but extremely effective, defined as "messages without words."

In a typical two-person conversation:

- 7% of the understanding comes from other person's word
- 38% from what we hear (tone of voice, vocal clarity, and verbal expressiveness)
- 55% from what we see/fell (includes facial expressions, dress and grooming postures, eye contact, touches, gestures)

A nod may carry enough communication, but usually re-phrasing the client's statement is the best way to show that we are following their train of thought and that we are quite interested in their ideas.

When we re-state the client's ideas, showing that we are trying to decipher the real meaning behind his comments, we show that it's important for us to take the time to listen and understand, prior to answering.

I have the benefit of my foreign accent. Clients might think that I am paraphrasing his words in order to process the message (in my less than perfect English). Going through this procedure is a good way to buy me enough time to formulate a logical, direct answer.

Sometimes, it really goes without saying

The full scope of a is composed of non-verbal sounds, verbal sounds and no sounds.

No sounds means – obviously – no sound. Silence. Something extremely important in communication, and usually not used well. When it happens to be used it is almost never intentionally. Of course you will not say each word with 5 seconds (or more) of silence between each, but then neither should you say each word with no silence whatsoever. Become aware of silence. Play with it. Experiment with it; Listen to what the silence tells your client about you and your expectations for him. Learn to use silence – long periods of silence and short periods of silence, even though the punctuation does not agree.

Non-verbal sounds are things like: snapping fingers, pointing at an object, raising the eyebrows (asking for input). Non-verbal sounds are usually used for emphasis or effect.

Verbal sounds are sounds made with the mouth. Sighs, hisses, groans, laughs and of course, words.

Words, otherwise known as "dialog" or "message", are deceptive things. For instance, let's take a three-word sentence – "He ran home." It is a simple, declarative sentence, right? What does it mean? Well, it means – some guy, He, did something, ran, to someplace, home. Correct? Well, yes and no. Let's try a little exercise.

Accent the first word, He. HE ran home. Now the sentence takes on the meaning that a particular person, HE (as opposed to all other possible people,) ran home.

Now, accent the second word, ran. He RAN home. The sentence now has a different meaning. Some guy did a particular action (as opposed to all other actions,) he RAN home.

Now accent the last word, home. He ran HOME. The meaning is again different. Some guy ran to a particular place (as opposed to all other places,) He ran HOME.

Three words that when stressed a certain way have a different meaning.

By controlling the dialog, you manipulate the audience and their reaction.

What are some of the ways one might manipulate the way a dialog is presented?

Here are a few:

Stress

Intentionally stressing specific words or phrases easily affects meaning. You should say your script, stressing different words to see how the meaning is altered each time, and how this would affect the way your client receives the message.

As you stress different words and phrases, keep yourself open to how the meaning is affected. Does one variation seem to emerge as assertive, or seem "right" in the context of attaining your client's agreement? Does one variation seem to create new revelations about your company, products or suggestions? Does it give new insights or a perspective you did not think before?

Pitch

Pitch has to do with how high or low your voice is. Pitch can reveal a lot about a person. A salesman that is afraid, agitated or nervous will often times speak in a higher pitch than they normally would. A person that is trying to project an air of authority or control might speak in a lower pitch than normal. Like with "STRESS", you should say your lines using different pitches.

Try saying you lines in a very high-pitched voice – as high as you can make it, even if it sounds ridiculous at first. Keep your mind open. How does saying the lines this way affect what you think about the meaning of the lines, the situation, and the core of the message? Now try saying the lines in as low a pitch as you can. How does it affect the general meaning? Say the same lines in a sing-song fashion, starting very low, gradually getting higher and higher, and then getting low again, repeating the low-high sequence over and over. Can you notice the difference?

Obviously, you will never have to present your message this way. This is an exercise to help you explore the full range of your voice. To help you use your voice to discover something about your selling power that you would not be able to discover by simply thinking about the possibilities.

Volume, Rhythm, Repetition and Diction

You are probably getting the idea of what you need to do to explore the full range of you voice. Go through your company's script, focusing on each of the elements, **VOLUME** (loud/soft and other variations), **RHYTHM** (fast/slow, and everything in between), **REPETITION** (repeat sounds, words, phrases, even if they are not written in repetition in the script), and **DICTION** (how precisely you pronounce a word).

With each element, explore the full range that you are capable of using. When exploring VOLUME, get loud – really loud then explore soft – really soft, and everything in between and various combinations. Use the same guidelines when exploring RHYTHM, REPETITION AND DICTION.

Your performance (sales presentation) should vary according to the audience

Personalization! It is a one-of-a-kind sales tool that provides you a unique selling style. It will provide you an understanding of the key buying motivators of each specific prospect.

There are many "selling do's and don'ts" for each stage in your sales cycle (Preparation, Demonstration, Conciliation). From these do's and don'ts, only a few are used in any given presentation, as a direct result of the client's specific needs, priorities, personal interests, and decision-making process. Identifying these items give us a valuable insight into the prospect's buying behavior to build a sales strategy that is certain to meet their "buying style" needs.

Adapting your presentation on a customer-by-customer basis, will, among other things:

- Increase your competitive edge by enhancing your prospects' trust and confidence in you.
- Increase your closing effectiveness.
- Reduce the number of contacts necessary to close a sale by capitalizing on tips and techniques to sell more effectively and strategically.
- Minimize price objections, by learning to communicate the value of a product in conformity to each buying style.
- Transform unqualified suspects into qualified prospects.
- Avoid having our most knowledgeable customers abuse us with severe pricing pressures and relentless negotiating (the extremely common "your price is too high.")
- Become able to negotiate with your customer on a financial level that will all but eliminate pricing pressures.
- Help you develop the knowledge and skill to effectively negotiate a complex sale.

- Set yourself apart from the vast majority of salespeople who reinforce the negative stereotype of high-pressure salespeople, by allowing your customer to feel safe and accept your advice.
- Develop in you a radar-like sensor that top professionals use to prevent dead-end situations.
- Make it easier to know how to judge the right time to bring in support people and when not to do it.
- Manage customer expectations with every sale and set the stage for referrals and repeat business.
- Eliminate surprises and disappointments for you and the customer.

Someone in the audience is not happy with the show; play it for the others, it's the fair thing to do

What's the worst part of a salesman's job? In most people's opinion is the high probability of rejection. Because people have the need to be accepted, rejection has a strong tendency to destroy our ego and hit us below the belt. Most salesmen have a way to deal with it (if they don't, they won't survive in their trade). Whatever they do, one thing they can't leave behind. Rejection should never be taken personally. Our client is rejecting our message, or rejecting the idea that they need the product or service. They are not necessarily rejecting us.

If we don't think of ourselves as a character in a play, we will fail to understand that they hate the message, not the messenger. Of course nobody makes a sale in every presentation, and rejection to our message is due to happen. Our reaction to it is the critical point here. Why bother if for every negative response there is someone ready to give us a positive answer. It's a question of not giving more importance to the fact than it deserves.

I don't believe there is an actor alive, even the extremely famous, who didn't deliver a less than perfect performance or received negative reviews for their work. It's part of life, and in my opinion, without rejection, how could we keep score of our success rate? In case of rejection, live through it. Give yourself five minutes to feel miserable (if it really means anything to you) and then – as they say in a Brazilian song, loosely translated – "stand up, beat off the dust, and go your way."

Tell the audience what you're going to do; do as you promised and explain what you've done!

In most performances this three steps message is to be used if we want consistently successful presentations.

1) We read about the play in the program, prior to the performance. One of its objectives is to give us a general idea of what to expect from the play and at the same time start to pump up our emotions in preparation for the event.

2) As we watch the performance, we hopefully get involved in the action, feeling with the actors the emotions of their characters.

3) After the show the critics give their opinions about the show and sometimes even have an effect on our original opinion.

In some way, these three phases should also present in a good sales presentation.

a) We somehow begin describing what they should expect. The clearer the message is the better. It's frustrating for the client, and counter-productive to the salesman not to establish from the start what should be the expectations on both parts. Imply that you are after the sale, that you expect an answer by a certain time and that he should try to analyze with you his needs and get ready for a decision.

b) In a professional manner, the salesman then presents his message, establishing credibility to the company, the service, the idea, and/or the product. The length of the message – just like in a play – depends on the amount of pertinent information that he needs to pass to the customer.

c) Under normal conditions there is no outside critique of a salesman's presentation, unless we consider the customer comments or the manager's evaluation (especially for rookies) as a review. However, after any presentation, successful or not, we should be looking for ways to improve, and new insights that could be used in future presentations.

Of course, very seldom anything can be done about that client's response, but learning from actual situations may improve future success rates.

A close friend of mine, when talking about public speeches always mentioned the golden rule for a good message: "tell the audience what you are going to talk about, deliver your message, and close by reviewing what you have talked about. The audience will get the point", he says, "even if they fall asleep during one of those three phases."

By experience I found out that customers may turn-off during some part of the presentation, so presenting the message in triplicate usually guarantees that they will get the main points.

Oscar winning actors give Oscar winning (successful) performances

There is nothing new in this assumption. If the performance is weak, the chances for Oscar are virtually none. Why, then, do salespeople expect successful results if their presentations are lame? The common excuse is "to save time". The common result is "saving commissions!" There is no way around it. It's an absolute in sales and a natural way to sort out the good and the bad professional.

When for some reason I am involved in a weak presentation, my only concern is the amount of time I wasted. I should know that unless a miracle happened, the final result would be anything but a sale. If sales (my main goal) was not a possibility, shouldn't I be golfing, or swimming instead? Contrary to what my friends think, I'm not workaholic. I wish I could afford not to work at all. But I chose to work so I can pay my bills, and the better my performance as a professional, the more bills I can afford.

I heard a few actors mention in interviews that after their movie was finished, they just knew it was Oscar material. I know the feeling. I have had presentations that were flawless and I was very happy with the whole thing. In a few cases, it didn't result in sale. Then, what? Personally, I don't have a problem with those few exceptions. I know I can't blame myself, and sincerely, I don't waste time trying to explain. It goes in my "X files" folder, as one of those things I can't explain, and it doesn't matter because they are not common at all.

My objective is to have more of those "Oscar winning presentations", knowing that it is a numbers game, and more often than not, I'm bound to cash big on them.

Does your character reflect your age?

As far as I am concerned, every age has its benefits and downfalls. Right now, a person may feel like he is in full bloom – and it feels good! They have tons of energy, but sometimes people might think of them as too young to take upon themselves some responsibilities. Upsides and downsides!

I always focus on the upsides of my age. I make whatever age I am to count for me, my family, and as many people as I can help. What about you? Do you look at yourself and say, "It's too bad I'm X years old." Don't do it! You will always be able to find some contrived excuse as to why your age works against you. Instead, focus on the positives! Sit down today and write out the five reasons why the age you are at right now is the PERFECT age for what you want to do. Then go make your age count for something!

Senior salespeople will be readily abundant in the near future. They also seem to be smarter and more goal-driven than their younger counterparts, according to many studies, where respondents gave the senior crowd high scores on qualities like knowledge of product and ability to meet sales goals. Also, contrary to popular belief, many are perfectly willing to put in long hours alongside their younger counterparts.

There are some myths that plague younger salespeople too. A young salesman can be experienced or well trained and age won't be a problem. Older salesman may be new in the career and not bring the results we would usually expect. Age is unimportant, irrelevant and shouldn't be taken in consideration when hiring a salesman.

As a last resort, if you really feel old, make sure the character you represent when selling is younger (maybe right at your favorite age bracket). Surprisingly, we can do that. And you will witness your clients actually believing you are as old (or young) as you portray yourself to be!

The basic tools of conversation

The following diagram seems obvious, but a closer look will show the arrows connecting the three separate elements as if they were one.

This means that the three elements, mind, body, voice, although separate, interact with each other. They communicate with each other. In fact, they depend on each other. Communication among the mind, the body and the voice is critical to the acting (as well as the selling) process.

Developing communication, a "conversation", among the mind, the body and the voice is an essential part of passing on a message.

The MIND is probably the element that tends to dominate most. Have you been in a small group where one person does almost all the talking? Not a heck of a lot of input from the other members of the conversational group. The person doing all the talking might indeed be interesting, entertaining and knowledgeable. If all you want to do is to sit back and be entertained, without contributing anything... great, then sit back, nod your head and say "uh-huh" once in a while. But the interaction would lack something. It would lack the depth, insight, color, ideas, personality and surprise that the other members of the group could contribute to the conversation, if they were given a chance.

Many salespeople, especially beginners, let their mind dominate the selling process. As a result, their performance lacks depth, insight, range, personality and surprise. It lacks input from the other members of the conversation, the body and the voice. It might even be a passable performance. But it lacks input from the other two important elements in the acting process, so it is sadly deficient.

Getting the conversation tools to work together

To explore, discover, and develop a character that will motivate your clients to pay attention to your message and accept your invitation to accept certain terms, a salesman must learn to encourage his voice and body to join the conversation.

Most people guarantee that every actor and salesman should have felt what is like to be hungry. That feeling is your body communicating to your mind, "Hey buddy, I need food. Feed me!" Your mind did not initiate this communication. Your mind did not say, "Hmm. I have not had anything to eat for four or five hours, I think I'll make the stomach grumble and hurt a little, get cranky, and I'll even start to think up food thoughts. OK stomach, start grumbling..."

Your body often initiates communication with your mind:

- Your stomach growls after a long hike.
- Your nose smells smoke, then you decide to look for fire.
- You see a big dog, hear him growl, you stop, then you decide it is wiser to walk the other direction – fast!
- You feel the warmth of the sun on your back at the beach and then you relax and feel happy.

Of course, once the mind is aware of something, it communicates back to the body to take a course of action:

- Prepare a bologna sandwich for lunch.
- Sniff the air and slowly seek out the source of the smoke
- Move to the other side of the street and keep an eye on the dog.
- Roll onto your back because your back is hot and you don't want to get sunburned.

This kind of conversation happens so quickly and so often, we hardly think about it. But it happens, and it propels us through each day of our lives. The salesman's job (just like an artist) is to encourage this conversation between the body and the mind, and to become as consciously aware of it as they can.

As I said earlier, the mind tends to dominate the acting process, especially in the beginning. There is a lot of thinking that goes on. Script analysis, character analysis, interpretation of relationships, detecting and blocking objection, reading the client's body language, all sorts of thinking. The conscious mind gets a real workout.

Rehearsal and role-playing is the place where a salesman can do his best work at getting the body involved in the conversation. Your body can't get very involved sitting in a chair reciting a script. You have to move. Not as conspicuously as an actor in a play, but get closer to the client, then get away. Move around to get samples, forms, pen, or sit back while the customer is presenting his ideas. This combination is crucial to bring the client to a full understanding of the message and, hopefully, full acceptance of the terms.

Don't shout and don't abuse your audience's (client's) tolerance

When my youngest daughter participated in the play "Annie", she portrayed one of the orphans. It was a good play (at her Junior High), but the sound that day, for some reason, was terrible. The drama teacher came with the solution (speak as loud as you can). The result: an interesting play, obviously, but very unusual. Whispers were said many decibels above humanly acceptable. So much attention was given to the "volume" of the voice, that the tone was forgotten, or better yet, destroyed!

Before the beginning of the second act the sound was fixed. What a difference. The songs were more natural; the tone of voice would vary from conversation to conversation. The audience could follow the message and emotionally participate. In contrast, we all spent the first act laughing about how everybody was making his or her best effort to be heard.

If we are not careful on a sales presentation, that's exactly what can happen. Our shouting will be the centerpiece of the presentation, and not the message itself. Be careful! Your clients may think the high volume implies pressure, desire to humiliate them, or lack of knowledge of your product or service. This is a mistake that can cost you not only the sale, but also the reputation.

Avoid the clichés

Everybody is unique. No questions about that. We think and act in ways that can easily be identified by those who closely know us. As a salesman, however, being mainstream, regular, average – in our use of words – is nothing to be ashamed of. Independent of our background, regional accent or other shortcoming, which we can't do much to avoid, repeating words more often than needed may sound annoying to those listening, but again can distract them from the "real" message.

Although the title of this book promises that we will re-examine some clichés, in our sales presentations they should be the exception more than the rule.

Words like: Eh… like… swell… you see… cool… darn… when constantly repeated makes the whole message dull, and dull doesn't usually sell! Clichés and exaggerations (This is the best product since sliced bread!) may sound fun and acceptable if used meaningfully, but in the end it may equal your product, service, and actually the whole presentation, with all the other junk in the market that argue the same cliché claims.

When we get involved emotionally, our normal reaction is to speak clearly. We still have engraved in our minds the TV footage on 9/11, on the streets of New York, as people were interviewed. They all chose the words to match the emotion. It was an event way too important to mess up the message.... They didn't go, "Oh, well, you know, it was a plane..." People were being almost Shakespearean because they were emotionally heightened. Our performance should be fueled by our emotions, and our script should include words that absolutely reflect the importance of the moment, and the uniqueness of our message.

Always send the audience the right message

Every salesman, at some point, was scared to death that a certain client would say no! As a result we "pretend" we are not interested in selling anything. Isn't that the biggest lie ever? Why would I go to the effort of presenting a product, service or idea, if I don't care if the audience is buying or not? Am I that stupid? What about the client?

As I have mentioned before, communication (actually, good communication) is the key in our presentation. I need to tell the audience (the client) exactly what I intend him or her to do. We can't send an unclear message and expect good results. The client won't "read between the lines" all the time, as we usually hope he will do. Do we need to twist their arm? Not really! We can be subtle and effective, insinuating and comprehensible at the same time.

Our allies in our quest to communicate the subliminal message (Buy! Buy! Buy!) are: the trial closes, the price conditioning and the expectation of sale. They deserve some attention:

Trial closes – the closed ended questions that we ask in order to provoke the audience to see themselves as a client. Some examples: Wouldn't you love owning one of these? Can you see an improvement in your personal life with the constant use of this product?

Price conditioning – defines to the client a "ballpark" figure that can make their price expectations a little more realistic when it comes to discuss price. Comparisons usually work best: A product like this usually costs thousands of dollars! Some people would pay over $5,000 for what we are offering.

Expectation of sale – the most subliminal of all messages, it tells the client that we know that they need, want and will buy our product or service, even though they might not be personally convinced. We just let our certainty be reflected in our comments: When (not if) you start using this product... Before we sign the contract, let me explain...

All three (the trial closes, the price conditioning and the expectation of sale) should be used as needed, to cement the idea of becoming a client in the mind of the audience. Everything else will naturally fall in place.

Triggering the logic with an emotional approach

Several surveys show that most sales reps and managers prefer a logical sales presentation. They say good data and the right supporting facts are the best way to persuade others to buy their product, services or ideas. Often, we present our supporting data and through logical steps lead the client to convince themselves to accept the information we are presenting.

Why do we insist in using logic and discarding emotion as the force behind our decisions?

Neuroscientists have recently discovered that the brain waves we emit when we engage in logical thinking (for example, when we solve a math problem) are virtually identical to those we emit when we are forced to plunge our hands and arms into icy water. It's painful! Further, these researchers have determined that we burn 4 times more calories for heavy thinking, compared with "mental cruising."

No wonder people hate a logical approach!

Luckily for us, our brains are hard-wired with mechanisms that help us make good decisions without painstaking analysis and reasoning. These mechanisms are known as triggers, but you can also think of them as "instincts" or "gut feelings." Essentially, they are decision-making shortcuts that we use easily and naturally. As a matter of fact, we often don't even realize we're using them!

Simply put, triggers are our navigational aids. They help us make easy, non-analytical, yet correct decisions. One example is the consistency trigger. Here's how it works. We all have a kind of database in our brains that records past thoughts and actions. This database provides a roadmap for future decisions. When faced with a decision, our brain does an instantaneous search, and we are oriented to act in a way that is consistent with past actions.

In short, we do what we've done before. A citizen who has voted for the conservative slate in the past will naturally do so again, without bothering to analyze the rhetoric of all the candidates running. Spenders make decisions to keep spending; savers tend to decide again and again to save. Cautious people take careful actions; careless people do not.

Now, what does this mean for sales reps?

Smart salespeople don't force their clients into icy water! Skilled reps don't demand from their clientele more energy to make a decision. They help their clients – by using proven triggers – to make good decisions. They make the effort to learn what their clients want, doing the heavy thinking for their clients, and determining how to position the presentation.

Some obvious triggers include:

Hope. Leads us to make certain decisions because a potential outcome is so attractive!

Reciprocity. What happens when someone gives us a gift or service? As the Tupperware people know, we often automatically return the favor by buying something.

Greed. Make your price seem as much a bargain as possible. The greater you make the perceived value, the greater the greed you'll evoke from your prospect.

Urgency. Come up with a solid reason why your product or service must be acted on right away. Provide incentives, reasons to buy now and strong calls for action.

Curiosity. Early in your sales presentation, use seeds of curiosity and promise a payoff that will cause a prospect to keep reading and/or pay attention.

Desire to belong. Determine the group of people who already own your product. Use the information to craft your sales presentation.

Skilled salesmen evaluate several triggers that will apply to a client. Then they carefully frame and deliver a presentation that is based on those triggers. They use facts and figures, when needed, to support a triggers-based decision.

The formula is fundamental: Sell with triggers, the client's navigation system for making correct decisions. Use facts, figures, and logic only when needed to reinforce a triggers-based decision. It may be the opposite of what you're used to – but it's a surefire way to win at persuasion.

Presentation is a track not a trail

A good friend of mine explained our presentations with this illustration that helped me remember his point clearly. In a railroad track there is not much room for variation. The train engineer can't decide to take the train out of the pre-set rail design. This should be our view of a sales script. We can vary slightly (speed, timing, etc), but we shouldn't allow ourselves to get derailed – which would literally mean disaster.

Unfortunately, some salespeople believe the scripts are trails in a forest. You can follow them, or for any reason just create a new trail (as long as you get to the destination – which is their justification of choice).

I heard some salespeople complain that going through a script shows a lack of professionalism, and that they would sound boring and monotonous to the client. This is a totally false assumption. The best professionals elect to use scripts, for many good reasons. Among them:

- Regularity, the knowledge that each client will be equally exposed to the message.
- Assurance that important parts have not been left out.
- Ability to follow a train of thought that will lead the audience to take some steps.
- Guarantee of not be carried away from the subject, by having a main course of action to come back to.

If we pay attention, physicians follow a script as they ask us some memorized questions: our sleep patterns, our diet, our life style, etc. Lawyers wouldn't dare to go to court without a very specific step-by-step script. Architects follow a non-written script when they check a blueprint (are there enough windows, lost spaces, color coordination, etc?). Why should sales professionals think they are above other professionals?

Only a few reasons justify getting off the script and "improvise": some points may not apply to that specific customer, or some warranties are not legal in that state. Usually, giving the whole presentation with little variation will avoid future misunderstandings. And we don't need to "remember" exactly what you said to a certain customer, because you have said the same thing to all of them, with no exception.

We are talking about a piece of art, not a sketch

It's just a job... or is it? It seems like a stretch to insist that salespeople should face their job as a work or art, when most of us think that it is just "survival". However, the way we view our job is meaningful, if we consider that it can affect the way our colleagues, our clients and superiors also regard us as a professional.

I don't have any statistics, except my own experience, but those who view their jobs as a "survival" will not get to the level of success they would otherwise enjoy. As a matter of fact, most of the time, they will not last as a salesman.

A wise person once said, "Anything worth doing is worth doing well." What job is more important (or worth doing) in the world today than selling? Politicians sell their image, nations sell their production, companies sell their products or services, and people sell their personality. Why take sales – as an essential job – lightly, when the whole world revolves around it?

The combination of all that is known, thought, felt and perceived about your company, service or product is called "branding". A company's marketing department spends millions carefully creating and projecting a "brand" image to differentiate your company and draw customers.

At the same time, what is the sales department doing?

Salespeople, as well as their managers, in some cases, are usually doing their own thing. In other words, the brand message is diluted or lost by the time it gets to the street.

Since "sales is an art" rather than a process, sales management and forecasting must also take the form of art. If a consistent process for lead generation, closing the sale and reporting the status of a pending deal does not exist, the sales forecasting process will not be a reliable predictor of future revenues. This will leave management poorly equipped to match the market's requirements with the organization's or the product's resources.

Should it come as a surprise that the top producers, as well as their wise managers do take the time to make the result of their efforts a masterpiece?

Don't focus on bad performances (failures); think about the standing ovations (achievements)

We all know a sales professional who can tell stories without end. They all like to brag on how they outsmarted a client, how they closed a deal considered lost, and how they helped a client to identify their needs and come to terms with the solution. This "know-it-all" behavior may seem unacceptable, but in reality is very healthy. It's a very crude way to produce self-motivation, but nonetheless it works.

The opposite is not necessarily beneficial. In general, the salesman that is only thinking about lost deals, weak presentations, dwelling on those failures for an extended period of time is really opening the door for even more failures. In the most disappointing cases they are always depressed (and depressing). There is a constant complaint about the economy, the unfair competition, the lack or customers, the colleagues' behavior, and other different alleged reasons that deep down are one and the same: excuses!

Even though it is good to learn from our mistakes, some of us see a bad day in our sales lives as a curse, a plague, and firmly believe there is nothing we can do to fix it. Waste your time complaining and you won't have any time left to be victorious. Usually one of two things will happen to these salespeople: they either become a mediocre producer or, even worst, they abandon their career all together.

High expectation always comes before high achievement. You have to dream big and think big to be great. Think little goals and you can expect little achievement. Think big goals and you'll win great success. The first ingredient of your success is to dream a big dream. You're as small as your controlling desires, or as great as your dominant aspirations. A well-known message says that once your mind stretches to a new idea it never goes back to its original dimensions. In sales, once you learn to dream big, fight for greatness and achieve success, anything less is unacceptable.

Forgive the audience, other actors (co-workers), the director (managers) or the performance (presentation)

The lack of forgiveness is a brick wall to your success. There are two situations in which we need to practice forgiveness:

One, we need to seek forgiveness if we have wronged someone. If you want to asphyxiate your future, leave someone out there that has some ax to grind with you. Rest assured, they would come back to haunt you (I am not at all saying this just pragmatically. We need to seek forgiveness because it is right, but there are down-to-earth ramifications nonetheless).

Two, we need to forgive those who have wronged us. When someone comes to you seeking forgiveness, we need to let him or her have it. To carry it on is to hold a boulder on our shoulders that will keep us from all of that we would attain.

Do you need to seek someone's forgiveness? If so, do it right now. Do you need to forgive? Let them know today that you have fully forgiven them. In doing this, we clear our path for success!

In many ways we become what we admire. We look at something and roll it around in our minds as something good and then try to emulate it and it draws us to become like it (or them). We can admire a character trait, a skill, or a person. Sometimes we will admire someone's purpose. Usually those traits or people who are most worthy of admiration are not those we would think of at first.

If we truly want to achieve balanced success in this life, we would be well off to find people who are truly deserving of our admiration. Then, as we admire them, we can have our lives shaped by that which we long to become. Find someone today who you haven't necessarily admired in the past. Think about those things in his or her life that are admirable. Then decide to work on those things in your own life. And if you want to double your blessing, tell that person (right now) what you admire about them!

Dealing with fear

Nothing in life is to be feared. It is only to be understood. When you dare to face the things that scare you, you open the door to freedom and success. Most of your obstacles would melt away if, instead of cowering before them or procrastinating about dealing with them, you would make up your mind to walk boldly through them.

Don't be afraid to take the steps you need to take to make those positive changes in your life. To fight your fears, you must act. Your fears increase when you wait, put off, or postpone. If you understood your situation enough, you would never be afraid. The attainment of your dreams (without apprehension about your fears) is but an action away. Fear is conquered by a resolute action.

By far the biggest fear of actors, as well as salespeople, is the fear of failure. It even has strange technical names (Atychiphobia or Kakorrhaphiophobia). Just like a mythological monster, it takes other forms, like the fear of rejection. Rejection – if feared – is the pathway to failure. While failure itself is real, the fear of it exists only in our minds.

Earl Nightingale's says, "You become what you think about." If that's true, why doesn't everyone think "success?" The answer is a combination of what we expose ourselves to and how we condition ourselves.

Unfortunately, we live in a world of negative conditioning.

The fear factor is in half of the ads we see. Ads about life insurance, anti-freeze for stalled cars, tires that grip the road in rain, brakes that stop to avoid hitting a child and security systems so your home won't be robbed. You become "fear-conditioned."

We are constantly reminded to carry mace, get a burglar alarm and be sure we have "the club". To make matters worse we now see police around ATM machines, metal detectors in schools, federal agents at the airports. We can always rely on the local news to spread the trend.

In the midst of fear we struggle for success. And while we fear failure – or at least don't want it around us – we all face it in one form or another every day.

Dealing with failure

Everyone fails. But, failure is relative. Its measurement is subjective. Mostly it occurs in our mind. If you avoid "I failed" and focus on "I just learned what never to do again" you've got a completely different mindset. The status of failure is up to you.

There are degrees of failure in sales. Here are some external ones:
- Failure to prepare.
- Failure to make a sale.
- Failure to meet a quota.
- Failure to keep a job.

These external (outside) fears, lead to internal (inside) fears; fears based on what happens when you fail or when you are close to failing. Your reaction to internal fear determines your fate. It's not what happens to you, it's what you do with what happens to you. Here are the typical reactions to failure:
- Curse it.
- Deny it (a nice way of saying lie about it).
- Avoid it.
- Make an excuse about it.
- Blame others (the easiest to do).
- Quit.

Failure actually only happens when you decide to quit. You choose your results. Here are some things you can do to avoid getting to the "quit":
- Look at failure as an event not a person.
- Look for the reasons, and find the solution.
- List possible opportunities.

- Ask yourself what you learned, and try again.
- Don't associate with other "losers" – find a successful person to hang around.
- Create a new environment.
- Get a new mindset.

3) Conciliation

	Qualification	Presentation	Negotiation
Rehearsal	QR	PR	**NR**
Performance	QP	PP	**NP**
Critique	QC	PC	**NC**

The audience analyses their decision with logic deductions

During the presentation, emotion is the fuel that moves the client to a decision. Emotion is a term for certain reactions and expressed feelings. It is derived from the Latin verb, *movere*, in which its meaning is "to move". Emotions move and direct us to take actions.

After the presentation, the client will enforce his decision and recognize it as a good choice or a regretful mistake based purely on logic. A wise salesman will intermingle the presentation with loads of emotion and sprinkles of logic. This logic foundation will cement the client's decision after the "warm fuzzes" are gone... The importance of emotion is such that everything you do in a must be emotionally significant to the audience.

In a few cases, however, logic plays a bigger role:

Larger Sales: Generally speaking, the larger the sale, the more logically customers tend to make their decisions.

After a Bad Experience: The remembrance of the past losses makes the buyer skeptical. Those losses can be financial, emotional or both.

Fear of Making a Mistake: Fear can also cause a buyer a lot of anxiety. A buyer who has made a bad decision in the past will be careful not to repeat the mistake.

A successful salesman knows that he can't be successful if after they leave the client's presence, there is nothing left to justify the purchase, to sediment the truths conveyed during the presentation and to motivate the client to enjoy his decision and feel good about sharing his positive views with others.

The audience is looking for honest, logic answers. They must understand afterwards what it was said and how it was meant. My rule of thumb is to judge if a client would be ready to sell the product to someone else. If that's the case, he got the big picture and I did my job.

Use tactics appropriate to the other character

A first-class salesman listens, evaluates each client's need and acts accordingly. Clients are as different as they can be, and have different needs. A wise professional seeks to ensure the best results for each individual client. In some cases we need to educate or guide them through the whole process, by giving our clients the personal attention each client deserves. Being genuinely interested in the overall well being of each client helps foster long lasting relationships.

To help our client to act in a certain way, we need to create a tactic, or a way to get the other person to do it "our way". We may go through the whole presentation trying to entice the client to make a decision. But even though our objective is the same with every client, the tactic to get there should be carefully tailored to each situation. We may sweet-talk, play on their sympathy, demand, feel sorry for ourselves, and give them a guilt-trip, all in a matter of minutes.

More than ever, trying to understand the peculiarity of clients from different cultures is becoming essential. Sometimes the salesman needs to go out of his way to avoid offending people of other ethnicities. Behaviors or comments that are acceptable or indifferent in our culture may be extremely distasteful in other societies.

Men from Hindu background usually prefer that we address them, not their wives, when presenting our messages. When dealing with clients from the Middle East, we should avoid using our left hand, which in their culture is associated with disregard either to the product or to our professional relationship. Hispanics want first and foremost to establish friendship, and in general don't care as much for the small prints or iron clauses in the deal, because they believe that a friend (the salesperson they decided to trust blindly) would never let them get into a bad deal.

The same is true for clients from different professional backgrounds. Engineers and lawyers want to read the long contract and usually suggest changes to the documents we present. Salespeople are easier buyers and in general offer fewer objections.

Even though there are many tactical possibilities as there are objections, it is to our advantage to list the most common and prepare a well-defined script that will provide a general answer to each of those situations. These "canned" tactics don't need to be used exactly as they have been written, but they provide a basis for a reaction that will sound natural, sharp and clever to the client.

The more difficult the obstacle presented, the greater the number of tactics we should utilize. The advantages to the actor of varying the tactics are many. On the simplest level, it provides crucial variety and avoids dull repetition. In a deeper context, it gives the salesman samples of successful answers that can be incorporated in future presentations, when similar circumstances arrive.

Changing tactics also provokes a new and different response from our scene partner, to keep the scene (presentation) moving forward. These assorted reactions and/or answers will usually guide us to an overall understanding of the client's exact point of view. One warning: make sure the tactics reflect professionalism, ethics and integrity on your part.

Acting (Selling) is persuading other people to accept the character's ideas (products, services) and to motivate them to take the recommended action

In a world where "politically correct" is the norm, sales have received the strangest definitions: "engineering agreement", "advisory persuasion", and "transference of ideologies", among many others. They may be true, as far as they go, and that's all.

I prefer my extended version: "Selling is persuading other people to trust your ideas, products and services and perceive the urgency of taking the recommended course of action."

The first options are acceptable, but they leave out the last step: action! Too many people define the selling process up to the point of completion and then leave it incomplete. A sale is not complete until the need is satisfied... completely!

Far too long, people have been teaching salesmen to sell, and tried to simplify the process. Many feel that all you have to do is develop an exciting and convincing presentation and present it. Others feel that all you have to do is go see as many people as you possibly can, and tell your story. All of these are valid but they don't go far enough. Therefore, all the sales training courses that implement these various concepts or parts of them are, by themselves, incomplete.

Selling is a complete process of satisfying needs and wants. Anything less is incomplete. In short, a sale is not complete until the salesman:

- Analyzes the prospect or customer, and their circumstances, to discover a need or a want,
- Educates the customer so he can recognize his own need and want,
- Presents a well-defined answer, (whether it be ideas, products or services), as the best way to fulfill the need or want,
- Takes notice, confronts and dissipates every objection (hidden or visible),
- Convinces the prospect or customer to take the recommended action (sign the contract, or order the product, service, or idea), and then,
- Take whatever follow-up steps are necessary, to assure complete satisfaction.

When all of this is done, the selling process has been completed; a want or need has been satisfied; we have engineered an agreement. This may seem a very simple process, but it surely isn't. People and emotions are involved; people are interacting with other people's feelings, thoughts and emotions, what makes it a very complex process to say the least.

Selling has been seen as a simple thing in prosperous times. On the other hand, during recessions, selling can be a lot more difficult. However, selling occurs in any situation. I dare to say that the market does not affect the amount of selling going on, only determines if the process will be simpler or more complex than anticipated.

Selling will vary from selling a simple tie, or perfume over the counter in a retail store all the way to negotiating peace in a war zone or bargaining the terms in a divorce. Regardless of the circumstances, the selling process takes place, and follows similar guidelines. We make the process complicated as an excuse for not taking the time to understand it.

Be it in prosperous or declining times, our ability to sell should not be affected. Needs and wants are still moving people into action. These needs and wants may be different from time to time, but they will always be the propeller to action.

Use your best shot and hit the audience hard

When you watch a good play, or a well-done movie you experience a feeling that tells you it was worth taking the time to attend the performance. The same could be true when we read a poem, or an epic, and even when we watch a carefully prepared TV show. If I may play with words, maybe that's why we call these productions a "hit". We feel their power, and we feel it hard.

During the presentation of our message to our clientele, at some point they need to feel that insight of knowledge about our product or service and a sense of acceptance to what we are presenting. The harder they get hit, the better. Here, as in martial arts, the element of surprise is fundamental. You know the end result, but the client may not. Go through the presentation tactfully, guiding them to the final "punch". Lead them to the central message or group of messages that will make them see themselves benefiting from your product, service or idea.

Doug Yeaman, a real estate guru that I respect tremendously, named this moment "crystallization". It is when our client mentally visualizes his needs being met. Even though it is just in their mind, they start enjoying the sense of fulfillment. If you watch carefully you can see their face, their body language, or both, reflect the fact that the lights went on and "they've got it!"

The downside is that the window of opportunity is usually narrow, and it can happen at any stage of the presentation, depending on the client's needs. Should other things distract us, and we may miss it. That also explains the need to go through the main points of our script, in order to give them a fair chance to get hit by this or that step.

Our objective is to keep reading from his reaction, find out when the message hits him and capitalize on that. Define what item caused the reaction and mention it a few times until the end of the message. If the initial punch had enough strength, we should be able to close the deal effortlessly.

Occupy yourself while you listen, think of what you would say, but don't say it (yet)

Good actors need to be focused, waiting for cues. In theater, everybody in scene knows the other actors line. Unfortunately it is not as simple in sales. The client will say things that we may not expect. He may even throw us a curve ball and get us worried about the best way to answer.

Just one thing to do: buy time. Our minds need time to process each move and the consequences of each one of them. As in a chess game, take your time! However, because in reality we can't take forever, our minds can be processing the objection, thinking of possible solutions while the client is still expressing their concerns or ideas. It may sound as a hard task, but it works naturally after a while.

One word of caution: We are sometimes tempted to find a solution, decide that is an acceptable one and immediately rush, interrupt our client and throw our idea, expecting an enthusiastically acceptance on his part. Very unlikely! It doesn't matter how good our card is, let's wait until the client tells us – with as much detail as possible – what cards he has in his own hand. A few times, we will see that he will get to a good solution on his own, or will give us additional information, which may make our first idea totally unusable.

One way to buy time is to re-phrase the objection and pass it back to the client in the form of an open ended question. If the client says the delivery time is too long, we may reply, "Why do you think you would need less than so many days to receive the product?" In most cases, while giving us the answer, the client will reflect that the urgency is a result or bad planning on their part, and will automatically recognize than he doesn't have the right to make us responsible for his mistake.

As always, patience is the key. Like a good actor, wait for the cue. Watch the timing. Convey your point directly, clearly and win the respect of your client. As a bonus, close the sale.

Great actors are inventive

It comes with the territory. An actor is forced to make any unusual situation be seen by the audience as part of the play. I once watched a play where the character was supposed to kill himself, in his bedroom, with a gun that was in a certain drawer. He reached for the weapon but someone forgot to make sure it was there. He was forced to ad-lib. He left the scene for a quick second, as if going to another room, and came back with a knife, exclaiming: "Nothing will stop me from departing from my stupid fate". He pressed the knife against his heart, articulated a scream and fell, lifeless. The other characters came in and the play continued naturally.

I wouldn't know about the gun at all, if I hadn't been invited afterwards to meet the actors back stage. That was the main theme of the conversation, which brought many laughs and taught me a big lesson about making an unexpected situation go unnoticed.

I have been in this situation many times. A specific form or document that, somehow, is not at reach, or a picture or product sample that is not appropriate for that client. What to do? Go desperate (please, don't even consider this possibility!) or improvise. Describe the sample that you didn't bring. Make up a form to replace that one, or set up a time where the form can be filled up and sign, but get out of the meeting with the sale. These little stumbling blocks are too small to overpower our focus on closing the deal.

Of course, being inventive is not an excuse for being unprepared. Double-check your material, the forms, and all the tools you may use during a presentation. In the heat of the negotiation the need to be inventive may be a handicap we can't afford to display.

The actor I mentioned was telling everybody backstage that he would never go in scene without checking all the prompts. He learned the lesson quickly. So should we!

Actors (sales professionals) must be courageous

Courage is a very important qualification for a salesman. Heroes do feel afraid, but they face those fears and succeed. Experienced actors do feel butterflies in their stomach before a presentation, but they go on stage anyway. We need sometimes to fight a client's objection with firm, logic and proven statements. Doing so demands courage in confronting a client, who ultimately will be generating our income.

We should have courage to say certain things, and courage to be silent. Courage to suggest a course of action, and courage to recognize we may not know beyond doubt that our recommendation is absolutely correct.

During a presentation there are a few times where we may need to encircle ourselves with courage, prior to opening our mouth. For example:

- When we first get together and it's up to us to make up the conversation.
- When we establish the benefits of our products, services or ideas.
- When we determine the client's needs and vocally report this to him or her.
- When we present price and payment conditions, despite his or her previous statements that he has certain budget limitations.
- When we ask for their business.
- When we need to deny some concessions that the client is demanding as a condition to do business.
- When we need to contradict the clients' myths or misinformation and present facts that will demystify their ideas.

Going out on a limb and tell the customer how far we can go and how much we can help certainly places us in a vulnerable position, but it will never, by itself, stop us from selling. Customer do consider us specialists in our area of expertise and they will respect us when we have the courage to deliver our message straight.

If you can't win, enjoy the bumpy ride

I remember going to a very funny play where a guy in the first row was talking all the time. The main actor probably felt offended by his disrespect for the professionals on stage and picked on this guy, by including him in a few jokes. We all loved it, but after the show the guy left the theater complaining. I remember thinking that even though he would bad mouth the actor forever, the actor actually had the last laugh. The gentleman kept quiet (and embarrassed) the rest of the show and we had a wonderful time.

In sales, as in show business, this is an extreme exception to the rule. The rule is that we should respect every single customer, and present our message to him with the hope that he will become a great customer. Once in a long while, however, we face a client that it doesn't matter what we do will disrespect our job, disregard our efforts and in some cases offend us. By itself, it doesn't bother me (and it shouldn't), but when the customer has a completely illogical set of objections, with the sole purpose to humiliate the salesman, I take advantage of a trick that will not get the sale, but will put me back in control of the situation.

Very carefully I explain that he doesn't seem to value my product, service or idea, and that although I respect that, his behavior will prevent us from working together. I make it clear that not working with him is not a major problem, as we can still part friends. Usually, he gets back on track or I just wrap up my presentation and leave with a winning attitude (although with no sales). In a few cases, other people in the room will act in my behalf and give him a piece of their minds, while I quietly enjoy the turn of events.

Let's understand the important point, and that is: THIS IS A VERY EXTREME COURSE OF ACTION. I believe one in hundreds of presentations go that sour. The key is always trying to save all of them, and if the client still insists in being a jerk, we, very professionally, establish the guidelines for working together. If it doesn't work, we deny them the right to work with us. And have fun all the way through the remainder of our time together.

Customer concerns should give room to urgency

Most actors will dream of the idea that their play or movie becomes a top-seller, a record-breaker, an award-winner. They expect an unlimited budget, talented actors, perfect reviews, and a long-lasting success! Obviously, not everybody accomplishes even some of these goals. There are always some stumbling blocks that most professionals need to overcome. The vital point is to overcome the obstacles, by actually using them as allies.

It's a common truism that a client starts buying when he says no! A good salesman will instinctively recognize the buying signals and gain commitment without "going for the jugular". It becomes necessary to be an expert at building rapport, discovering needs, demonstrating value/benefits and highlighting uniqueness. The emphasis should be on effectively closing the sale and creating a customer for life!

When dealing with clients that present concern after concern and at first seem to make your job difficult, understand that they are really allowing the salesman to use those objections to build a counter-offensive that usually cannot be contested by the client:

Define the concern – Identify each of the barriers the client is presenting.

Develop Solution – Work out a simple solution best suited for the situation.

Deliver Solution – Present the solution to the client, in simple, direct terms.

Demonstrate Effectiveness – Describe how that solution can produce positive, measurable results for our clients.

If we develop the patience to really understand the objection, and present our product or service as the answer to those concerns, the apprehension in our client will evolve into urgency. They will now be excited about benefiting from our product or service, which wouldn't have happened if we couldn't address the objections accordingly.

When is it enough? Don't overdo it!

I remember a specific time (in my rookie years) when my sales manager asked us to role-play. We were supposed to overcome certain objections. I thought I did a good job, but was criticized for overselling. The presentation had been taped and I watched it a few times and found out exactly where I failed. This experience helped me to become self-conscious. Many years since that experience I still watch for signs of trying to sell to a client that is already sold into the product, service or idea. What a trap it can be!

A client is ready to close when he recognizes the need for that item, and expresses the fact that there is nothing that is stopping him from signing a sales contract. This is the moment where we don't show any more samples, don't describe any other benefits, and don't mention any lines in the script that we may have forgotten.

If I could consider over-selling a vice, I could honestly say I have had a hard time overcoming it. I like what I sell, and in the heat of negotiation, I seem to over-stress the value of the product I'm selling. I may go on and on defining the benefits, the warranties, and the superiority and so on. In the few times where I didn't watch it carefully and felt in this trap, I usually lost the deal, or needed to work harder to save it.

How do I know when enough is enough? By using trial closings. A few times during my presentation I should create opportunities to make a close-ended (yes or no) question and measure the level of acceptance. As the client expresses genuine acceptance of a given principle, it's time to go on. Doing that throughout the presentation will minimize the objections and get them ready for closing.

I would dare to say that over-selling is almost as damaging than underselling (i.e., not giving the customers enough facts, so they can make an informed decision).

The best critic of your job is yourself

In show business we sometimes need to wait until the following day to hear or read the critic's review. Those hours can be nerve-racking. And once the word is out, there is not much you can do to change bad reviews. Unfortunately, critics have the power to make or break a career. And sometimes there is no remedy for a misjudgment on their part. Their opinion seems to be final and supreme.

Evidently there are no professional reviews for sales presentations, unless we do it ourselves. I like to tape-record one of my presentations, every two-months or so, and analyze it in details, to find ways to improve my performance. Most of the time this is the only way to have a critic's point of view.

We can't count on our clients because they don't know what an ideal presentation would be in order to compare. We can't depend exclusively on our manager, because he can't be present in every presentation in order to judge its value. I don't trust third party critiques, unless the person was present, and has at least my level of product and company knowledge. Criticizing with responsibility is too complex to be made in the dark.

A good advice is to take a few minutes after each presentation and analyze what was discussed. Without the pressure of the client's presence it's easier to pinpoint any mistakes or anything overlooked during the sale. Constant – and honest – critique and consistent improvement, whenever necessary, are, of course, the key for success. However, it does take courage (to be critics of our own work) and integrity (not to "cover" or justify our mistakes). All the successful people do it, be it in the theatrical or sales atmosphere. And the more they do it the more they identify their shortcomings, overcome their limitations and discover their strength.

Interacting with clients after the show (sale)

When the curtains close, the audience wants to see the actors, shake hands, get autographs, and show their appreciation as fans. Let them! Being accessible after the show (closing) creates loyalty, admiration and respect.

Studies show that acquiring a new customer costs 7 to 10 times more than selling to existing customers. Why would any business or salesman not want to do everything they can to retain their existing customer base? With reasonable effort your customers will remain loyal and dedicated to you.

It's not sufficient, however, to simply care for your customers "just enough" to keep them from complaining. If you simply keep your customers satisfied, you may only get marginal results. Nowadays, customers are so used to poor service and performance that they have learned to accept mediocrity as the norm. Marginal service will yield marginal results. Consequently, the loyalty and commitment to you will be minimal. Your clients will migrate to another competitor as soon as they see a better offer.

On the same token, when they discover that you can offer outstanding service, they will automatically assume that your competitors can't even get close to it, and their loyalty is now at your disposal. We need to realize that the relationship begins at the first meeting, and does not end when the sale is completed. It is after the sale that you have the opportunity to shine and show the customer what you really are all about. Once the deal has been closed let your customers know that they've chosen the right company to do business with ... yours! A thank you note, a follow-up call, a message of success is all they need to get from an unmatched salesman.

Your customers should be so happy with your service, support and attention that they actually tell other people about their experience with your business. If you take really good care of your clients, they will not give your competitors a chance. They will come back year after year, helping your business to grow continuously.

Find your ideal audience ... focus on them, listen to them, and pinpoint their needs

The message in the play determines who will have interest in watch it. Under normal circumstances, adult themes do not appeal to children and chick-flicks do not appeal to most guys. Many small businesses have failed to determine whom their best prospects are, where those prospects live or how to reach them effectively and efficiently. This is a critical first step in any successful marketing strategy.

Their hope is that by presenting their generic message about their business to the greatest number of people, the result will be a higher number of sales. Effective marketing does not work that way.

The fact is, in most cases only a small percentage of the readers, listeners or viewers of mass media will have a need for your product or service at any given time. Some business owners may have a hard time believing this, but nevertheless, it's true. Not everyone needs or wants your product or service. Shocking, uh?

By not targeting your marketing to your very best and logical prospects, you are wasting most of your marketing dollars on people who have little or no interest in your product or service.

If there were only 100 true prospects for your product or service out of 10,000 possible readers of a publication, why would you want to spend thousands of dollars presenting your message over and over to the 9,900 non-prospects? Yet, this is the method most small business owners choose because they don't know that there is a much more cost-effective and profitable strategy.

Also important is the fact that you should never stop using something that is still working, because you, your employees or your friends are bored with it. Henry Ford once told an ad executive from his advertising agency, "It's time for you to come up with a new ad campaign. We've been using this one for too long and I'm sure the public has to be bored to death with it." Ford was reportedly miffed to hear, "But sir, we haven't even started running this campaign yet. The public has never seen it." Having seen the campaign presentations dozens of times, **he** was bored with it. **He** wanted to see something new and different. In successful and profitable marketing you should only be listening to your customers since they cast their votes with dollars rather than opinions.

If at first you don't sell, try, try again...

Effective salespeople know that persistence and repetition are vital for success. As I mentioned before, the sale begins when the customer says "no." But too many business owners spend a great deal of time and money attracting prospects to their businesses and then either follow-up with them just once, or, even worst, never follow-up with them at all.

Successful salespeople know that most of the sales are made after the seventh or eight call. Few are made after just one call.

Your prospects have many reasons for not buying from you immediately. They may not be ready to make a decision. They may have more pressing things on their minds. They may not feel comfortable enough with you, or trust you enough to buy right now. They may have more questions about your product/service, that haven't been answered. Or, they may have information from you and two or three of your competitors and are sincerely trying to determine which company would be their best choice.

By following up repeatedly, you will have a dramatic advantage over your competitors, since few of them will follow up more than once. When your prospects are ready to buy, which could be one week from now, or six months from now, you will have a better chance of getting the sale if you are uppermost in their minds. You can only do that by consistently following up.

Word-of-mouth referrals are an extremely important element of any business's marketing success. But most small businesses are making a big marketing mistake by believing that those referrals will come automatically. It's true that if you provide good service and your prices are competitive, you will probably get some word-of-mouth referrals. But to generate a highly profitable level of referrals takes more initiative and effort.

Bear in mind that unless someone comes to us and specifically asks for our recommendation of a good dentist, doctor, veterinarian, insurance agent or auto alarm specialist we are probably not going to actively promote these businesses to our friends and neighbors. How often in any given year are you asked to recommend a good dentist or an insurance agent? The chances are . . . not very often, if at all. That's why expecting referrals to come to you just by chance (as most small business owners do), is a fatal marketing mistake.

The most fatal mistake of all . . .

Conclusion

I admire many public figures and look up to many less-known heroes. Someone special that I really admire is Irving Berlin. He symbolizes us, immigrants, who, for centuries, have contributed to the growth and strength of America. He didn't need to declare his love for this country. It was constantly reflected in his work, his message, and his productive existence.

Irving Berlin was born Israel Beilin on May 11, 1888. One of eight children, his exact place of birth is unknown, although his family had been living in Tolochin, Byelorussia, when they immigrated to New York in 1893. When his father died, Berlin, just turned 13, took to the streets in various odd jobs, singing for pennies, until he became a singing waiter in a Chinatown Cafe.

Although this book is not about Irving, he reflects much of what salespeople and artists stand for. His love for his adopted country is legendary. His actions were acknowledged with the Army's Medal of Merit from President Truman in 1945, a Congressional Gold Medal from President Eisenhower in 1955 and the Freedom Medal from President Ford in 1977.

On September 22, 1989, at the age of 101, Irving Berlin died in his sleep in his town house in New York City.

Just like his patriotic music, the trade or sale of goods, services or ideas are a sure way to support the economy, improve our overall growth and maintain our country's singular position in the world market. The incredible similarity between the Broadway lifestyle and a salesman daily activity can be defined (with deep apologies to Irving Berlin) by a parody to his success "There is no business like show business", from Annie Get Your Gun (which opened on May 16, 1946, ran for 1,147 performances, and was the third longest running musical of the 1940s).

With a catalogue of over 1000 songs, Irving Berlin epitomized Jerome Kern's famous maxim that "Irving Berlin has no place in American music – he is American music."

There's no business like sales business
Like no business I know
Everything about it is appealing,
Products that clients think is hip
Nowhere can you get that happy feeling
When you're following a winning script.

There's no people like sales people,
They smile when they are low
Even with a sale that you know will hold,
You may be stranded out in the cold
Still you wouldn't change it for a sack of gold,
Let's go on with the show

The butcher, the baker, the grocer, the clerk
Are secretly unhappy men because
the butcher, the baker, the grocer, the clerk
Get paid for what they do, but no applause.
They'd gladly bid their dreary jobs goodbye
For anything theatrical and why?

There's no business like sales business
And I tell you it's so
Visiting with the clients is so thrilling,
Competing for a closing day and night.
Smiling as you watch the client agreeing,
And sign the paperwork without a fight.

There's no people like salespeople,
They smile when they are low
Deals come from everywhere with lots of sweat,
And when you lose them, you just go back
Where would you get money with no ceiling cap?
Let's go on with the show

The schedule, the weather, the dress code, the flu,
The manager that lifts you when you're down,

The headaches, the heartaches, the backaches,
The flats, the old car that decides to let you down
The big sale when your heart beats like a drum,
The appointment when the customers won't come

There's no business like sales business
Like no business I know
You get word before the day has started
That your favorite uncle died at dawn
Top of that, your pa and ma have parted,
You're broken-hearted, but you go on

There's no people like sales people,
They smile when they are low
Yesterday they told you that the market sucks,
That night you sold a million bucks
Next day on sales meeting they'll curse your luck,
Let's go on with the show!!

The struggles of our profession, as well as the highlights of a career as old as time itself will always be there. The honor or participating in a sale, be it retail business, international trading, or peace negotiations in the heat of war makes this profession one of the most honorable and at the same time one of the most misunderstood. It may always be like that, but...

THERE IS NO BUSINESS, LIKE SALES BUSINESS, so let's go on with the show!

Topics

About the Author

Nilton M. De Macedo, was born and raised in Rio de Janeiro, Brazil, where he graduated from Rio de Janeiro State University, majoring in Mass Communication, with minors in Marketing, Publicity and Public Relations. He received his Master Degree in Education (Elements of Adult Teaching) at the same institution. Since 1983, he has been involved with sales, mostly related to real estate.

He immigrated to the U.S. in 1986, with three toddlers along with his five-month pregnant wife, and chose Utah's Weber/Davis County area as their new home.

For 11 years he was Vice President of Marketing for a food supplement company, promoting their products exclusively to health professionals throughout the U.S. and twelve foreign countries.

In 1997 he went back to his passion – real estate – where, upon applying his knowledge of sales in the American market, he became "Rookie of the Year", as well as member of the President's Club (for high sales volume) every year since.

An unexpected invitation to open a Brazilian franchise for an American Real Estate company took him back and forth to his native city. For 18 months he single-handedly projected all the training material and established two real estate offices, which brought a new standard to real estate in South America, including a combination of personal notes, which became the backbone of this book.

Currently he has returned to his real estate company of choice, being a monthly recipient of the company's "Top Ten Club" award.

www.ingramcontent.com/pod-product-compliance
Lightning Source LLC
Chambersburg PA
CBHW030008190526
45157CB00014B/1205